Best Wishes

Other Books by Kohn

Best Wishes
For Common Days and Special Days

by

Harold E. Kohn

Illustrated by the Author

William B. Eerdmans Publishing Company
Grand Rapids, Michigan

Dedication

To Nina Wilson
Inspiration and Friend

Preface

It takes a certain audacity for a person to write any book, let alone his tenth volume. This book, like its nine predecessors, was written and illustrated with the same boldness that motivates all writing for publication, all preaching, teaching, and all the fine arts when they are at their best. It is the daring faith that something has come to a person that he should share: he has something too good to keep. It is not the belief that this good comes *from* him, but *through* him.

Writing such as this is done for the same reason we read: we write and read so that our minds may enjoy vital contact with other minds. In writing, as in reading, one reaches out and has fellowship with persons he will never see, in homes he will never visit. And in these moments of vital communion the writer happily passes along good that has come his way.

This collection of brief meditations on life's meanings ranges widely. Here are essays exploring the significance of some of our great holidays, others dealing with man's ancient, yet ever-current problems of confusion, insecurity, discouragement, fear, guilt and grief, finding resources for life's management and for growth. Some treat such varied subjects as self-expression, open-mindedness (wise and unwise), what Christ means to Christians and the joyful celebration of life. The book derives its title *Best Wishes* from one of this volume's meditations on life's highest values.

In his famous "Review of the Dictionary" humorist Bill Nye said that the author had a splendid vocabulary and seemed to possess ready grasp of the meaning of many words, but Nye felt the book lacked much of a plot and the author changed the subject too frequently. At first glance the last point may seem to apply to this book. Each small chapter, like a bead, has its own shape, size and identity. Yet there is a string upon which all the beads of meaning are strung. They are threaded on the theme of what the Christian faith has to say to those who are trying to get their bearings in a bewildering world.

7

The author's "best wishes" to the reader include the hope that something said in these pages may illumine the way that leads at last to the Father's house.

THANKS

My efficient and loyal secretary, Twilla Kayner, has — with characteristic good cheer — typed the manuscript without a single complaint about my nearly undecipherable handwriting. She has my gratitude.

My wife, Marian, who is more delightful companion than flaw-seeking critic, has kindly read these essays, corrected galley proofs and, with a rare genius for tactfully pointing out a blemish, has made valuable suggestions for improving this book. Moreover, she has lightened my task of writing with her encouragement and her faith that possibilities for good rest in these efforts.

I am greatly indebted to Ed Grade, S. George Little and Rex Barley of General Features Corporation for permission to use here articles I originally wrote for newspaper distribution by General Features, an affiliate of the Los Angeles Times Syndicate.

Dr. Curtis Chambers, formerly editor of *Church and Home* magazine, now merged with *Together* magazine, has been gracious in granting permission for including several articles from that publication.

And finally to William B. Eerdmans, the publisher, and Calvin Bulthuis and Cornelius Lambregtse, editor and book designer, who have been good friends as well as co-laborers in book production, and to kind readers without whom every writer is hopelessly frustrated this author expresses his enduring appreciation.

To all of these a hearty thanks and *best wishes.*

— HAROLD E. KOHN

Contents

9

Part 1
Meditations for Common Days

Autumn Days

1

The Sacrament of Walking

Charles Lamb contended that those who give thanks only before meals are missing many precious opportunities. "I am disposed," he declared, "to say grace upon twenty other occasions . . . I want a form for setting out upon a pleasant walk, for a moonlight ramble, for a friendly meeting, or a solved problem."

I especially agree that grace can be appropriately said before taking a walk, for walking in an alert, open-minded manner can be a significant experience with high spiritual value, rather than a reluctantly accepted means of getting from one place to another. As the celebration of holy communion is more than consumption of bread and wine, and holy baptism is more than the application of water to a person's body, so holy walking is more than mere travel on "shank's horses." Like every sacrament of the Church which takes hold of our vagrant, wandering thoughts and focuses them upon the deepest meaning behind some familiar object such as bread, wine or water, so meaningful walking concentrates attention on what lies beyond mere body movements. It is an alert adventure of the human spirit into the near-at-hand, in the faith that our most commonplace surroundings will surrender riches to the inquisitive mind and reverent soul.

Sacramental walking means sauntering. Henry David Thoreau, who journeyed little beyond Concord, Massachusetts, was onetime asked if he traveled much, and he answered, "I have traveled widely in Concord." His walks were intensive exercises of an alert and penetrating mind that observed more of interest in Concord than many men would see on a world tour. Thoreau derived the word "saunter" from "sainte terre," meaning holy

13

land, because, for him, taking a walk *anywhere* meant a pilgrimage to the Holy Land that lay spread around his feet.

Sacramental walking, then, is dedicated to seeing the good and the beautiful near our doorstep. It is the art of investigating the ordinary in the glad belief that it will yield extraordinary treasure. It is the certainty that beauty abides in a dewdrop captured by a cobweb on your backyard shrub as much as it resides in the grandeur of the Alps or Mount Fujiyama. It is the assurance that at any moment neighboring wild birds will present you a private concert as memorably thrilling as any command performance of a royal choir.

Rostand, the French dramatist, shed light on the romance of living when he wrote, "The man of romance is not he whose existence is diversified by the greatest possible number of extraordinary events, but he in whom the simplest occurrences produce the most live sensations." Our familiar surroundings can be experienced with such probing curiosity, appreciation and gratitude that even a daily walk to the same nearby place will never exhaust the possibilities for excitement and wonder.

Moreover, sacramental walking stretches beyond the glory of ordinary things. It involves living on tiptoe, with the expectation that somewhere just beyond us lingers some event about to happen that has never occurred before and may never take place again, and could change our entire life.

It was on an "ordinary" walk near our home that I saw my first pileated woodpecker, a bird many of my neighbors have never seen in a lifetime of looking. And it was on another "ordinary" stroll near our house that a friend and I were surrounded by six baby weasels who were doubtlessly on their first spring outing with their mother (since they had not yet learned to obey her frantic warnings that they were approaching danger). We were sniffed at and thoroughly investigated before the lithe little fellows satisfied their curiosity and scampered away. This had never happened to me before, and is unlikely to happen to me or anyone else again, but it did occur on an "ordinary" walk, on an "ordinary" evening, when my companion and I entertained only "ordinary" expectations of a leisurely ramble to our gate and back.

One might even find God, or be found by God, while walking. It was while walking on the plains of Midian, near Mount Horeb, tending his sheep, that Moses turned aside to watch a burning

bush and heard God's call to lead the people of Israel out of Egyptian bondage. Moses mingled wonder and reverence with his walking, and that walk and its after-effects changed world history.

Read the Gospels carefully and see how the ministry of Jesus was related to walking. It was while on a walk that he

15

called disciples: "As he walked by the Sea of Galilee he saw two brothers . . . casting a net into the sea: for they were fishermen. And he said to them, Follow me, and I will make you fishers of men." (Matthew 4:18-19). John the Baptist looked at Jesus as he walked, and said, "Behold the Lamb of God, which taketh away the sin of the world." (John 1:29). In the vivid, imaginative language of the book of Genesis, God is thought of as practicing the art of walking. Adam and Eve are pictured hearing "the sound of the Lord God walking in the garden in the cool of the day." (Genesis 3:8). One of the most heartening promises made to Israel was "And I will walk among you, and will be your God, and you shall be my people." And it was said of Enoch that his passing from scenes of earth was simply a continuing walk with God: "Enoch walked with God; and he was not, for God took him." (Genesis 5:14).

Sacramental walking is companionship with the Eternal, a journey of discovery of the God who is always near, revealed in all His works, but too seldom recognized by our jaded souls which have looked at too much and have seen too little.

It is a holy use of the imagination, pretending we are strangers on the earth, who have never before seen one of God's birds in flight, or heard a wren's gay song, and have never before seen a tree, or felt the texture of its bark, or listened to a child's shrill cries of delight at finding a baby toad, or a flower bravely peeking through a crack in the sidewalk.

Sacramental walking means learning to walk all over again, learning to focus attention, learning to see again, hear again, smell again, touch again, learning to turn the familiar over in one's mind and see it anew.

Sacramental walking means knowing the present moment of casual movement over our little patch of the good earth is a precious gift from God. And it means squeezing every drop of soul-nourishment from it.

2

Big World; Small People

Many people become despondent because they feel utterly lost in such a big world as this.

The Psalmist, who knew little about the shape and size of the earth, and next to nothing about the heavens, wondered aloud, "When I consider the heavens, what is man that thou art mindful of him and the son of man that thou visitest him?" How much more astonished at God's concern for man would he have been had he been exposed to the view of the universe revealed by modern science! The British scientist, H. Spenser Jones, has pointed to the earth as an infinitesimal atom in the vast spaces of the universe. The earth and moon are so small and the sun so great, says Jones, that if our earth were placed at the sun's center, the moon would be only half-way to the surface. Yet, if our sun were placed at the center of Betelgeuse, the brightest star in the constellation of Orion, our earth could swing in its vast orbit around the sun and never reach more than half-way to the surface of that giant star. And if that fact is astonishing consider this: in the galactic systems to which the earth, the moon, the sun and Betelgeuse belong there are some two hundred thousand such stupendous suns. Furthermore, this galactic system is but one of some seventy-five million universes that astronomers have thus far discovered. It is small wonder that some people are tempted to accept H. L. Mencken's estimate of man: "Man is a sick fly taking a dizzy ride on a gigantic flywheel."

17

Three correctives are needed for our feelings of insignificance in a big world governed by a God too busy with the operations of a universe to give attention to one individual human being.

First, we must rid ourselves of the false assumption that bigness and importance are the same thing. In a world where we value a small diamond more than a big lump of coal, a small home filled with love more than a big house filled with hostility, a small child more highly than a big automobile, it should not seem strange that God cares more for any one of us than He does about the disappearance of a star from His heavens. If we, at our best, do not confuse size with value, why would God?

Second, a better conception of God's goodness and greatness is needed if we are not to despair over our seeming insignificance. Too often we assign to God our own limitations. We find life so overcrowded that we have little time or interest for small details that need our attention. So it seems the same must be true of God, and we — who are but small details in an immense universe — must certainly escape God's attention and care. Or we become so engaged in big business that we neglect our children, and we foolishly imagine God has the same problem in managing His universe. Or we maintain an interest in masses of men, such as the hungry of India or the unevangelized of South America, and we let institutions do our charitable or missionary work for us, while we merely furnish the funds. But we take little time for individuals. This failing we project upon the nature of God.

But God does not have man's failings or limitations. God is infinitely better than our very best. There is enough of the love of God for everyone, and it comes to each one as if God had none other to consider.

Anyone who stands on a lakeshore on a bright moonlit night witnesses a parable of God's love for the individual. The silver ripple of moonlight runs over the water directly at that one watcher of the night as if he were the only person on earth. But another night wanderer standing on the lakeshore three miles away sees the moonlight coming his way, as if the flood of beauty were meant for none but him.

The moon brightens the entire landscape and illumines all who walk in its trail of light. Yet it shines for each spell-bound onlooker as if it were intended for him alone.

Again, anyone who eats an apple tastes a parable of God's

18

care for the individual. For although the sun has a million grain fields to encourage toward harvest and countless gardens and orchards to bathe with light and warmth, the sun ripens each apple as if it had no other tasks to perform, as if its entire energy could be given to that one fruit. So with God. Every person has his own unique place in God's pervasive purpose and love.

3

New Roots in Old Channels

Foresters have discovered that pine trees grow better in forested land than when planted in open meadows or abandoned fields. Pines started on uncleared forest soils achieve greater size and hardiness to withstand winds because their roots follow old root channels and strike deeper into the ground. As roots of a young tree grope toward the heart of the earth the tip of the tree stretches farther heavenward, and as roots penetrate into old channels and expand in the roomy space previously prepared for them by trees long gone, the entire tree is strengthened and stabilized against days of adversity and testing.

One of the many advantages of knowing the history of our faith, being thoroughly acquainted with the Bible and the creeds, the lives of the heroes of ancient Israel, the Gospel stories of Christ and the saints of the early Church, is that such knowledge, rightly used, enables us to send the new roots of our souls into old root channels. Our thoughts burrow into the big questions that confronted men of old: "Where is thy God?" "Canst thou by searching find out God?" "Where is thy brother?" "If a man die, shall he live again?" "What shall it profit a man if he shall gain the whole world, and lose his own soul?" "Is it lawful to give tribute to Caesar?" "What think ye of Christ?" "Why seek ye the living among the dead?" We discover how God's people answered the searching questions, and we learn what

they did with their anxieties, tensions, guilt - consciousness, lostness, loneliness, their feeling of frail finitude and brooding death - consciousness. We discover how they found answers, and *the Answer,* to their problems and needs. And we search in these likely places for the satisfactions they found. When our roots penetrate old root channels our spirits grow to an extent otherwise impossible.

Using old root channels does not mean we believe Biblical truth is stale or static, and that new revelation is unavailable to us. And it does not mean an unthinking acceptance of our inheritance from the past, a casual, mindless acceptance of creeds and catechisms at their face value. Indeed, such careless assent is irreligious rather than devout, for it ignores the commandment to "love the Lord your God with . . . all your mind," as well as "with all your heart, and with all your soul

... and with all your strength." (See Mark 12:30.) The words of the Bible and the witness of the Church should never close our minds, but open them. They should not do away with individual investigation, but stimulate it. When we come to some new understanding of the Word or the creeds our exclamation should never be "I have arrived," but a restless "I must be on my way!"

Attention to the witness of the devout souls of ages past means rediscovery of what has made life most worthwhile to the best of men of all time — an experimental awareness of the greatness and goodness of God. In the history of our faith, then, experience has preceded doctrine. Then, through doctrine, the faithful have attempted to announce, define and explain experience. For example, Pentecost, with the coming of the Holy Spirit into the lives of the apostles, is the root of Church teaching about the Holy Spirit. We should always remember what the early apostles so well knew, that while it is important to have the right *opinion* about the Holy Spirit, it is possible to have the correct opinion and none of the *power* of the Spirit. We are more likely to celebrate Pentecost than to experience it. Using old root channels means plunging our souls deep into the experience of Power and Abiding Presence that the early Church called "Pentecost."

Walt Whitman illustrates our thought. One time "the good, gray poet" listened to an astronomer's fact-filled address about the heavens, the location of the planets, the stars and their constellations and the glory of a star-lit night. "I began to feel tired and sick," Whitman said,

> Till rising and gliding out, I wander'd off by myself,
> In the mystical moist night-air, and from time to time,
> Look'd up in perfect silence to the stars.

Life offers no satisfying substitutes for that kind of knowing. Information about the stars will greatly enhance and deepen appreciation of the night sky, but no lectures on astronomy or learned books on the subject can take the place of a star-bath, when the soul is cleansed of earth's dust by soaking in the vast stretches of God's universe. Such an experience is radical. It goes "to the roots," rediscovering for oneself what thoughtful, reverent men have always felt when they have stood in the star-drenched silences and have thought of the baffling distances, the

21

wondrous beauty, the littleness of man and the greatness of God.

So we should always be restless with mere information, opinions, doctrines and creeds about God, as important as they are. There must come times when we rise and "seek His face," and sit at the feet of His Son, and feel the surge of His Power. Then we are "radically" Christian in the best sense.

Then our roots find old channels, and the soul can climb to towering heights.

4

An Autumn Letter to a Friend in Grief

DEAR FRIEND:

Only a few hours ago I learned with sadness of your husband's sudden passing. My sorrow is for you, rather than for him, because he is all right now. He lived fully, effectively, serving the world well, and he is now in Good Hands. But you and your family have been sorely hurt by the wrench of his unexpected departure and by the loneliness that gives grief its aching anguish.

I pray that your Christian faith will support you now with the assurance that death is not fatal to our loved ones. It cannot destroy them. It only fulfills them, so that all that is partial becomes complete, all that is but seed becomes flower, and all that is imperfect becomes perfected.

If we had our choice as to when we would die, many of us would choose an autumn day, for this is a time when our passing would seem natural and appropriate. The unquiet busyness of summer is past, and all things that have had their brief hour of growth are now ripened and fulfilled. Autumn is sweet with harvested fruits. Now the colorful leaf drifts to its bed, a kind of sacramental act signifying resignation and obedience to a Power beyond itself. Swallows have clustered and have sped southward. Wild geese now fly in wedges toward their winter homes. And above all else, late autumn is a time when we dream of coming holidays and of homecoming.

In these days of autumn beauty it is some comfort to know that we are all a part of a plan that autumn symbolizes. The passing of a dear one is a sacred reminder that our brief stay here is intended for the nurture of our souls, for growth and maturing, and when seed becomes flower and fruit, and when the fruit of life has ripened, God has other, higher purposes for us. As the leaf returns to the soil from which the parent tree has come, as migrant birds feel the tug of a distant home and fly toward it, as we all are drawn homeward at holiday time, so the soul has a destiny toward which it moves. Death is the fulfillment toward which all human life secretly, unconsciously yearns. Death is homegoing. So we all rise and follow the homeward call that sounds in our souls as softly as a half-heard sigh.

Has death come to your loved one too early? Does death *ever* come too soon? Nearly always death is premature for those who must bid a loved one "goodbye" for a little while. But death can hardly come soon enough for those who say "hello." You know how it is when large families gather for holidays. Some travel by automobile, some by bus, some by train and others by airplane. How they get home matters little as long as they reach their destination safely. Many get home when expected, but there is often one who especially gladdens the hearts of the folks at home by arriving a day or two earlier than planned.

In a similar way, sometimes one of our loved ones gladdens those already in our Eternal Home by arriving earlier than expected. While those he has left behind for awhile suffer grief sooner than they intended, those he greets at our Father's House, and the traveller himself, rejoice at the glad surprise of his early arrival.

May God comfort and strengthen you and yours with the assurance that in His good time He will translate all earth's grievous "goodbye's" into glad greetings of "hello."

You are in my love and prayers.

Affectionately,
Harold E. Kohn

23

Winter Days

5

Growing Every Day

Now, in winter, when trees are stripped of their foliage, the bark on their trunks shows clearly how greatly trees expand as the seasons come and go. On most of our common trees, such as the maple, oak, elm and ash, the bark splits to allow the trees to grow. The "healed" cracks make a textured roughness on the trunks of these giant plants. The elastic bark of white birches has no such vertical breaks in its surface. It simply expands with the growth of the trees. When the bark finally snaps, it falls in long banners that flutter in the wind.

What I admire most about a tree is that it continues to grow until it dies. All creatures change from day to day, but all change is not growth. Decay, too, is change. The botanists tell us a tree grows as long as it lives, daily adding breadth and height to its stature. Daily its roots draw sustenance from the soil, and daily it drinks moisture from the air and absorbs light and energy from the beneficent sun. Wind, rain, snow and ice contribute to its tough character.

The Psalmist said of the righteous man, "And he shall be like a *tree* planted by the rivers of water." The expression is apt, for a chief characteristic of a tree and of the life of faith is perpetual growth.

America's greatest folk hero, Abraham Lincoln, was not always heroic. Once he was nearly as unprepossessing in personality as he was physically ungainly. As a young man he was easily depressed, moved to morose glumness and to sullen silence. He made serious, though sincere, mistakes which he later regretted. But Lincoln grew.

There was a time when the sensitive Lincoln could not have shrugged off the misunderstandings, name-calling and slander that fell upon him during his Presidency. When a member of his Cabinet was reported to have called Lincoln a fool, the President replied, "He must be right; he is a very smart man." As a young man Lincoln lacked the grace to respond habitually with such ready tolerance and forgiveness. Early in Lincoln's life he could not have felt, let alone spoken, the imperishable

25

words of his Second Inaugural Address, "With malice toward none; with charity for all. ..." He was not always good enough, wise enough, great enough to feel or think or speak that way.

Lincoln stood tall in spiritual stature as a youngster. He was taller still as a young congressman, and a giant when he was nominated for the Presidency of the United States. But Lincoln was never spiritually tall enough to please Abraham Lincoln. He grew all the days of his life.

What are the conditions of growth? How is spiritual growth encouraged?

Dissatisfaction with self, when it is creatively used, is a growth stimulant. Growth comes from the recognition that we do not know everything worth knowing, that we have not achieved everything worth achieving, and that we have not become what we ought to be.

Growth comes from a certain openness, a porousness, like the roots of a tree that absorb nourishment from the surroundings. Growth rises from hospitality to beauty, truth and goodness that are not our own, making them into our own. This means careful consideration of viewpoints that are new to us and differ from ours. It means a willingness to be disturbed, upset, changed. All conversion starts here, and all growth.

We grow when our spiritual income exceeds our expenditures.

Growth in spiritual stature and strength is encouraged by association with other people who are also seeking to grow, just as trees are strengthened, and stabilized and stimulated by intertwining their roots with the roots of neighboring trees.

Acceptance of big responsibilities tends to excite growth that is sufficient to handle them. We should accept our share of this world's troubles without fear, resentment, or self-pity. The art of growing is not one of dodging trouble, but that of using it as food for growth.

We grow as we improve our habits, substituting good habits for bad and still better habits for good ones. The holy habits of regular, set times for meditation, private devotions, public worship, writing notes of encouragement, making visits that bring cheer and help to the needy, all of these, and more, add to our stature.

We need a standard against which we measure our growth. A molehill must seem great to an ant. Little hills appear to be

26

big until we see the mountains looming beyond them. Mountains seem great until we measure them against the stars. A Christian may feel sufficiently tall while standing back to back against his neighbor. But let him stand face to face with Christ and he recovers his spiritual perspective.

Before the father of William the Conqueror left for the Crusades he compelled his barons to swear allegiance to his young son. The barons protested, "He is but a child." The father answered, "He is little, but he will grow." The Christian is a mixture of humility and hope. He knows he is little. He is sure he will grow.

6

Ties That Bind

When you shovel snow from your sidewalk, only a few square inches of your shovel actually touches the snow, but in reality every molecule of shovel, handle and the snow shoveller, too, is engaged in the task. The energy expended flows from far beyond your hands and shoulders and back and legs to the calories of heat you consumed in the orange juice you had for breakfast. Moreover, the history of that energy can be traced beyond the orange juice to an orange, to a grocery, to a wholesaler to an orange tree in an orange grove, to the sun and to the Creator who fashioned the sun and the heavens from which it shines.

When you carry wood for your fireplace, or plant a garden, or write a letter or clasp the hand of a friend, or act in any matter whatever, that particular action is but part of a long chain of interrelated energies and influences. Every act we perform possesses this wondrous union with powers beyond our ordinary awareness.

So it is with our spiritual nature. No person is really self-made or self-sufficient. We are linked with other people, and every thought and deed is connected to, and influenced in some way by, earlier thoughts and deeds of folks near us and remote from us, our contemporaries and men of other centuries and civilizations.

One richly meaningful word we use to denote these inter-relationships is "fellowship." It means the state of being associated with others, and it refers to the many ties that unite us — family, friendship, community, education, church, labor, business, industry, recreation, international relations. We are all blessed because of such relations, and sometimes cursed by them. They are the source of joy, and of suffering. These far-flung, complex relationships reach across geographical, religious and racial boundaries, enabling a white child in Nevada to be healthier because he eats fruits picked by Mexican and Negro harvesters in California and Florida. A Roman Catholic lad in Chicago drinks milk furnished by a Protestant dairyman in Wisconsin. A middle-aged Protestant in a New Orleans hospital is saved from death through brain surgery performed by a young Catholic surgeon who was trained at Mayo Clinic in Minnesota. A Gentile farmer in Iowa is kept warm by woolen garments manufactured by a Jew in New York.

The network of interdependence also reaches across boundaries of time. Human relatedness makes it possible for a twentieth century American to enjoy freedom purchased by the blood of eighteenth century patriots. It permits a child in Canada, bitten by a rabid dog, to live today because of the discoveries of a long-dead French scientist, Louis Pasteur. It makes it possible for a Vietnamese soldier to survive a wound because of 'the work of a Japanese scientist, Kitsato, who long ago isolated the bacillus of tetanus. It makes it certain that millions live more courageously, hopefully, trustfully now because of words written by the Psalmist thousands of years ago, because of words preached by the Galilean a few hundreds of years later, and because of letters sent from prison by Saint Paul a few years after Christ graced the earth with His presence. Fellowship makes it possible for us to know with the help of others what we could never know alone, and to become with the help of others what we could never be by our own unaided wisdom and strength.

Yet our relatedness makes for misery as well as blessing. A stranger's cough on a New York subway train or an airplane flying over Illinois spreads germs and viruses among fellow passengers, who in turn carry the infection to still others in an ever-widening circle.

An automobile factory labor strike in Detroit, Michigan, causes a small parts manufacturer to shut down his plant in Ohio, throwing scores of men — who have never seen Detroit — out of work.

An airplane crash in Arizona widows a woman in Newport, Rhode Island.

A bartender in Washington, D.C., sells a customer from Virginia one drink too many. The drinker drunkenly drives his car onto the highway and slices into an oncoming vehicle, killing a man whom he has never met before, making a widow of his wife and his three children fatherless.

How should we live in a world of such intricate and vital relationships?

First, we should live with discretion, choosing carefully those influences in our lives that we want to underscore, emphasize and strengthen. The trashy and trivial will meet our eyes and din in our ears, and the sordid will sometimes claim our attention. This we cannot avoid. But we *can* determine what we will hold long and lovingly before our minds, what we will intentionally savor, value and deeply absorb.

Good living, like good art, consists of drawing a clear, firm line somewhere. It means deliberately choosing the things that will influence us most. Through the Bible and other sacred books, through great literature, music and art we can have fellowship with the most splendid souls of all time. The chief principle of spiritual and intellectual growth lies in making wise choices as to what and who will most influence us.

Second, we should live responsibly. If those near me and others beyond my reach influence my thought, behavior and general welfare, it is just as certain that what I am and what I do affects others.

Because rapid transportation and communication and a crowded world have blended men into a closer community, we live in an age of unprecedented responsibility for the welfare of others. If we fail in being all we can be or in our assignments of duty, some part of humanity will be hurt by our negligence. If we succeed in fitting into the plans of the Great Designer and perform our tasks nobly, the world will be better because we have been here for awhile.

One test of the good life is the depth and breadth and richness of its intentional involvement with other people. The man whose interests and affections are profoundly involved with his family lives on a higher level than does the "loner," who absents himself from his home at every opportunity. The person who cares deeply for his community and contributes to its general welfare lives on a higher plane than does the fellow who attempts to withdraw from all community life because he has "enough to keep me busy at home." The man who is knowledgeable about world affairs and who extends his sympathy and active help to the hurt and needy of the world has risen to higher spiritual achievement than has the person who believes that "charity begins at home," and *remains* there.

The blind hero of Hugh Walpole's *Blind Man's House* almost destroys all happiness and peace in his home with his haughty, unyielding pride and his emotional detachment from his family. But he comes to his senses at last and expresses new insight in these words: "I have learned this lesson of our interdependence, the lesson all mankind must learn. No one of us can move anymore, or sigh, or sneeze, or cough, or whisper without disturbing the rest of us. Until we learn this fellowship, generous and understanding, of all living men upon the earth, there will be no peace."

For better or for worse we belong to each other. The man of faith is dedicated to seeing that his human relationships are for the better, for the sake of self-improvement and for the sake of his family, friends and community, and for the good of the world.

7

The Last Thing I Want
Is Security

One thing the wild creatures of the North most certainly are not — they are not "secure." They do not possess what superficial observers of nature sentimentalize as perfect tranquility. They know the tortures of hunger, the weaknesses arising from disease and misery, the anxiety of being hunted, the pressures of the chase. Although moments of comparative relaxation are enjoyed, much of a wild animal's life is spent under strain, seeking a fleeting security, hunting enough food, a safe shelter, protection from his enemies and assuagement for his hurts. The constant struggle keeps him alert, vigorous and vital.

Even though this has been a comparatively mild winter, reports of starved deer are beginning to trickle into the newspapers now that food reserves in many areas have been used up. Most deer reach the lowest point in the annual weight-curve in late February or early March, just before spring arrives. When the average temperature is below forty degrees the weight of last spring's fawns tends to follow the trend of the temperature: the lower the temperature drops the more weight they lose, even when the best foods are available. This is because a great deal of the body energy is required simply for keeping the deer's internal temperature normal, even if one disregarded the energy required for moving deer about over the snow-covered landscape. One big-game biologist discovered that when the temperature drops much below 30 degrees Fahrenheit, deer lose from three to twelve pounds per 100 pounds of body weight a week, no matter how nutritive their food may be. Winter in the North is a long contest between deer and frigid weather. Often coldness wins.

When spring and summer come the struggle to stay alive continues. Lungworms infest approximately one-third of all whitetail deer. Nose bots infect the nasal passages of our graceful Northern neighbors, feed on the mucus and sometimes choke the deer. Liver flukes, stomach worms, tapeworm, footworms

32

and numerous other parasites contribute to the deer's misery and sometimes to their death. Injuries become infected. Later the hunting season takes its toll. The idyllic life the sentimental nature-lover supposes forest royalty enjoys is purely imaginary.

What is so of the deer is true of all other inhabitants of field and forest. Injury and disease, predator and scarcity make life anything but "secure," and the more one explores the kingdom of the wild, the more apparent it is that living nature is a realm of tension rather than security.

In these times of extreme tension, personal and political, there has been an upsurge of publications offering cheap and quick "security" for those suffering from tension. In the United States some of these books have become best sellers, and for a reason: no nation is more problem-conscious and strain-ridden than the United States. Someone has said, "America is no longer a melting pot — it's a pressure cooker!" Such books will continue to sell, because our appetite for peace of mind is well-nigh insatiable. We shall continue to look for "security" from life's problems because there is no finding it either in nature or in human society. The publicists for security will always have a limitless market. Insecurity of some sort has always been with us. It is as much a part of this world as are atoms and molecules, earth and water, snow-covered Northland and sun-flooded tropics, deer and man.

In this Age of Anxiety the "peace of mind" cults are enjoying a field day with propaganda which invites people to perfect happiness and complete freedom from tension and care. Suddenly there has sprung up a whole new clergy composed of ministers of the Gospel of Relaxation. They have summarized the Scriptures into "Blessed are the peace-finders for they shall have normal blood pressure" and "Take up your tranquilizers and follow me." They conveniently forget that the Christ who dominates the Gospels was often disturbed, "a man of sorrow and acquainted with grief." His disciples were problem people who misunderstood Him and some deserted Him. He wept at a friend's grave, and sweat blood as He agonizingly prayed in Gethsemane. Far from dying peacefully "without a struggle" and "in his sleep," He died of the worst physical torture and while praying compassionately for his enemies. There was nothing limp about Him!

Human nature requires a certain tautness. Those who never

suffer fatigue cannot taste the sweetness of rest; those who face
no problems cannot experience the joy of a surprising solution;
those who have not been misunderstood and who have never
had an enemy cannot savor the wonder of reconciliation; those
who have never sensed guilt cannot know the release of full
pardon; those who are not disturbed about a sick and tormented
world will do nothing to alleviate the physical and spiritual
hurts of their fellowmen; those lacking in compassion will be

wanting in usefulness. Freedom from problems and freedom from care are about the worst curses that can befall us.

A tensionless existence is well-nigh meaningless. A completely relaxed person has about as much worth to the world as a completely relaxed mainspring has to a watch. The power of a mainspring is in its capacity for tension. Have you ever heard anyone play a violin afflicted with loose strings? Relaxed strings produce noise, not music. The violinist purposely produces tension in the strings; only then can the instrument sing.

What kind of peace is it, then, that God offers us? What does the Bible mean when it says, "The peace of God, which passeth all understanding, shall keep your hearts and minds through Christ Jesus?" The peace of which the Bible speaks certainly does not signify freedom from problems, nor does it imply that God is a kind of Celestial Trouble-Shooter whose main business is to make life easy for us. While the peace prescribed by the tranquility sects is self-centered, aimed at getting what we can from God, the peace to which the Bible witnesses is God-centered, and derived from our dedication to God. It arises not from God's being our device, subject to our manipulations, so that we can put in a prayer and out pops a blessing. Peace comes from the recognition that we are His, owned and cared for by Him. As one old colored saint explained his trustful spirit, "I jes' looks up and prays, 'Lord take care of yo' property.'" We are property with problems of wear and corrosion, problems over which battles are waged and upon which the rains fall and the floods come, but we are God's property, and it is cared for, and His ownership will be proved and His love and will for it will triumph at last.

Peace of mind in the midst of great wealth, good health, wide recognition and acclaim, and smooth paths everywhere — that is understandable. But the "peace that passes understanding" is the trust that people have without all these.

There is a place in God's world for care, concern and compassion (literally to "suffer with," to feel another's pain in your heart), and a place for peace. Our cares, concerns and compassions keep us spiritually alert and spur us on toward usefulness. And although the peace that comes from being His does not make us "secure" from life's multiform problems, it allows us to deal with them with the assurance of victory here or Hereafter.

35

Spring Days

8
Shallows and Depths

Most bodies of water that delight our eyes vary greatly in depth. Our little brook gaily races over amber, sun-drenched shallows. The crystal stream lightly ripples over stones, playfully teases the whirligig beetles and water striders that play on its surface, trying to upset them with a frenzied burst of speed. But the brook also has somber, quiet depths where brook trout and rainbow trout lie, where ducks pause for a morning swim, where birches and balsams are reflected in tranquil pools.

Not far below our south fence the stream rolls into Lake Charlevoix which, in turn, through a series of linkages with small bodies of water is joined to nearby Lake Michigan. Lake Charlevoix is one of the Midwest's largest inland lakes, having an area of almost twenty-four square miles, and depths of ninety feet and more. But it has shallows, too. Where the water is only inches deep, water lilies hold their clean cups to the sun and little waves whisper secrets concerning timeless things, and carefree breezes play tag among the sedges.

Mighty Lake Michigan, one of the world's largest lakes, lies off to the west of us only about five miles away from where I write. Is Lake Michigan shallow or deep? It is both. Along the shore of this great body of water there are places where tiny minnows dart amidst sparkling ripples, where small shore birds wade among the rocks hunting for insects, where changing skies are reflected in the magnificent silver-blue mirror. Then, again, midway across Lake Michigan, and just opposite the entrance to Green Bay, a deep, dark pocket indents the bottom of the lake, plunging to 923 feet beneath the surface. Lake Michigan is shallow and deep, depending upon where you look, and its variety of depth is part of its beauty and charm.

So it is with human nature. Some people derisively say of a person, "He is so shallow," or exclaim admiringly of another, "He is such a profound person." Such judgments are only partly true, at best. Few people are entirely shallow, having no deep desires whatsoever, no profound loneliness, no abyss of mystery, no seemingly bottomless trouble.

And no one is equally deep all over, any more than is our brook, or Lake Charlevoix, or Lake Michigan. Even the best person, like the deepest ocean, has his shallows, his moments of humor, light laughter and musing — when his mind is at play. God made His children, as He fashioned the waters of the earth, with a variety of depth — ranging from shallow to profound.

It is a primary concern of the devout soul that he does not confuse the shallows with the depths. The profoundly troubled Psalmist, remembering how the snows of Mount Hermon melted and dashed down the steep walls of the mountain, likened the echoing and reechoing of the waterfalls to man's questioning and God's response, to man's prayer and God's answer, to God's call to man, and man's reply: "Deep calls to deep at the thunder of cataracts." (Psalm 42:7) This is true. As every man of faith has found, the depths do cry out, and from the Depths a response does come. Man prays. God replies with ready help. Or God speaks to the sensitive soul through Scripture, the Word spoken from the pulpit, through historical events, through nature, through a disciplined conscience, through the wisdom or example of a friend, and the attentive soul makes an appropriate response.

But it is just as true that a similar communication occurs between the shallows in man and the shallow things of life. A humorous situation, or a story related by a friend, strikes us as funny and we laugh. A trashy drama appears on television and we give it little thought. Silly commercials on television, radio and billboards get only a superficial consideration from us. Golf, baseball, swimming and other forms of recreation have their places in our lives, but — if we are well balanced — no sport has a prime importance, taking the place of family or God. Recreation is a secondary interest, eliciting a secondary response. One of the worst things that can happen to a person is to mistake the call of the shallows for the call of the deep, and to give to superficial matters a wholehearted, devout response.

And another tragic response is that of answering the call of the deep with a shallow response. Marian Evans Cross, the most distinguished of English women novelists (whose pen name was George Eliot), was very much attracted to the sociologist and philosopher Herbert Spencer. For years Spencer toyed with the woman's affections. Finally he took a coin and flipped it. Heads he would marry her, tails he would not. The coin came down

38

tails up, and Spencer did not marry the lady. That superficial response to marriage labels the man as shallow where he should have been deep. One of the curses of modern society is that when the profundities of life's most intimate human relationship call, many men and women answer from the shallows.

So with our treatment of children. A society that is more concerned about the horse-power of its automobiles than the character of its children, a society that shows more concern for gleaming teeth than for shining souls, is one that has its shallows and depths confused. A society that gives first-rate attention to second-rate matters and second-rate loyalties to first-rate causes desperately needs to ponder and heed Christ's one-sentence sermon on values: "Render to Caesar the things that are Caesar's, and to God the things that are God's."

That which chiefly distinguishes the life of faith is its different and courageous valuation of things. What the world holds dear — money, fame, sensational pleasures, freedom from responsibility — the dedi-

cated spirit sees as secondary, at best. And that to which the world is indifferent or lukewarm, or sees as secondary — the search for God's truth, wonder at the beauty and mystery of the universe and the goodness and grace of God — the devout soul holds dear.

Perhaps the way God measures us is by our responses. When the shallows call do they receive the shallow answer they deserve? When the deep calls, does it get a worthy response — from the depths?

9

Stones and Songs

I removed rocks
And fallen logs
From our little stream,
And the brook
Lost its laughter
And forgot its song.

Then I understood
Why, when I prayed,
"O Lord,
Take all my troubles away,"
The answer came,
"Are you sure
You want this,
My child?"

10

Afraid of Shortages?

Now in mid-spring the trees of North America awaken to the call of returning birds and to the choruses of spring peepers singing in the marshes. Sap rises, bringing renewed life to each tree, like blood recommencing circulation in a numb leg that has "gone to sleep."

The tender light of April has coaxed green leaves from dark buds lining barren limbs. Hills have removed their heavy, white winter coats and have put on light scarves of green. City parks and countrysides are freshened with an emerald mist that has settled on the treetops.

All across the land orchards clothe their naked limbs with a super-abundance of leaves. Horticulturalists estimate that it takes thirty leaves to make a Jonathan apple and fifty to produce a big Delicious apple. (About thirty leaves are required to make a large peach.) However, mature apple trees will be equipped with about one hundred thousand leaves apiece, many more than each tree will need to produce its fruit or to do its work of lifting out of the earth four gallons of water per tree each hour. This abundance of reserve leaves is to make the tree adequate to any time of crisis. Succulent leaves will attract many insects. The larvae of moths, butterflies, sawflies and beetles will attack and consume foliage, reducing the tree's capacity for manufacturing food. So each healthy tree produces a total leaf surface that is far greater than its anticipated need, so that if a considerable number of its leaves are destroyed, the tree can still survive.

All through nature a tendency can be found to produce reserves. Quail, pheasants, ducks and other ground-nesting birds lay more eggs than are necessary to perpetuate their race, so that if some eggs are destroyed by marauding crows or plundering skunks or mink, enough will survive to compose a small family. A female brook trout may lay five thousand eggs to assure the preservation of the species, since some eggs will be infertile and many young will be prey to other fish and will

41

not live to see their first birthday. Nature insists upon reserves to assure continuation of the race.

When man is wise, he too plans upon an abundance of reserves. Merely enough strength to "get by" will never do. When the cables were built to support the weight of the San Francisco-Oakland bridge, they were fashioned with capability of bearing a load two and one-half times as great as the maximum they would ever be called upon to bear. That is the way to handle all of life. All bridge builders should provide more strength in their structures than they will ever need. All scholars should know more about their subject than any examination will demand. Every long-distance runner needs a "second wind," a reservoir of energy to draw upon when other men's power wanes. A healthy person is one who has more physical reserves than any active day can drain and more than life's crises can exhaust.

What we all greatly need is not a diminishing of problems, but an increase in adequacy. Speaking of his disciples Jesus said, "I am come that they might have life, and that they might have it more abundantly." Abundant life is no mere "hand to mouth" existence with barely enough caring, forgiveness, patience and love to get by. Abundance of spiritual life means more than enough power for common daily needs, plus inexhaustible reserves for any crisis that may confront us.

The person who has the abundance of life Christ came to bring us can spend virtue lavishly because his resources are plentiful. He can care for people unreservedly, the people near him and all over the earth, people of his own creed, color and nationality and those of other faiths, races and nations, because his resources of care are attached to the limitless reservoirs of God's care.

He can afford to be slighted, shunned, hurt, because he has enough forgiveness in his heart for any crisis that comes his way.

He can be patient when other men's patience is exhausted because he not only has his own patience to draw upon, but God's patience too.

He can squander love upon the undeserving and the irresponsive because he knows there will always be more love where the last love came from.

An English poet and essayist, while pleasantly talkative among close friends, was restrained among strangers and casual acquaintances. When a woman complained that he did not readily engage in conversation, he replied, "I have only ninepence in ready money in my pocket, but I can draw a check for a thousand pounds!" He refused to put all his wisdom in a showcase. He had much in reserve.

The Christian faith is one of abundant resources. The man of faith does not need to count on little bits of cash in his spiritual pockets. He can write a check for any amount needed on the account of "God and Company." That account is inexhaustible.

11
Why We Wither

A few days ago I was invited into a living room where I was shown a bouquet of yellow lady slippers, which are members of the orchid family of flowers. They are spread widely over North America. Only a few hours before these shy, lovely blossoms had nodded to the moist breath of cool woodland breezes. Then some intruder had invaded the hiding place of these wildflowers and had plucked them from their roots. Almost as soon as they were picked, the shining beauties began to lose their freshness and grace and to wilt and wither. Before many hours had passed, the yellow ladyslippers were but poor, brown mementoes of the bright blazes of wild grace that once had warmed a woodland glade.

One of the prevailing fallacies of our time is that we can sustain blossoms and keep them alive and fresh without their roots. This is especially so concerning a so-called "Christian civilization." Many would like to believe that such a civilization can flower and remain vital without being rooted in Christian beliefs. This is impossible. How can a civilization based upon a continuing struggle for moral responsibility, justice, peace and goodwill among men, survive if it is cut off from its roots, which are beliefs that every person everywhere is a child of God, and should be treated as God's child?

A civilization is more than dynamos, machines, sky-scrapers, industry, commerce and competition, compassion for the poor and the mistreated. Civilization is a state of mind and spirit that produces such things. The material and spiritual advantages of our generation will at last be doomed if severed from the beliefs that make them possible. If our social order is to be to any degree Christian, it can only be because it is based upon compelling material things to serve the spirit of man rather than seducing the spirit to serve material things. Apart from Christian insight and belief there can be no Christian action or social order.

Psychologist Henry C. Link once said, "All the material advantages of our civilization conspire to make our lives easier and our characters weaker." Being "better off" does not mean we are really better. If we produce and increase wealth without a growing wisdom, intensification of human contacts without deepening human understanding, bigger weapons without great determination to help rather than hurt, then all the blossoms of "Christian" civilization are doomed to die because they are cut off from the roots that sustain them.

Our great fear today is not of guided missiles but of misguided men. A better tomorrow will depend upon better men and women for tomorrow. And better men and women will depend upon better beliefs.

What we have just said about civilization is true also of one's individual life and character. Occasionally we hear someone say, "What does it matter what we *believe* as long as we *do* what is right?" Of course it matters, and precisely because what we do rises from what we believe. Belief is the root of action.

Dr. Samuel Johnson was one time told that an acquaintance of his, a renowned cynic, had loudly professed to see no difference between virtue and vice. Dr. Johnson was astonished at the man's beliefs, and advised, "If he does really think there is no distinction between virtue and vice, why, sir, when he

leaves our houses let us count our spoons!" Dr. Johnson's precautions were sensible. We tend to act out what we really believe. Belief is the root of life. Action is the blossom.

The roots of Christian conduct are in Christian belief and dedication. If we want to improve conduct we must begin by improving the qualities of the basic beliefs to which we are committed. We must be like the alfalfa plant, which many farmers use for hay; it sends its roots deeper than almost any other cultivated crop. An alfalfa plant only two or three feet high has been known to extend its roots to a depth of fifty feet in search of nutriment and water. It is this tendency toward long roots that makes alfalfa a good soil builder and enables it to survive drought. Its greenness and vitality depend upon its roots.

If we want our spirits to survive the blighting effects of foul moods, anxiety, brief spells of meaninglessness, and the temptations of a growing materialism in society, we must send our roots deep into the nourishing, vitalizing convictions that God is good, that He cares, that He is near, and that in Christ He gives all the light to live by that we shall ever need.

12

What Jesus Christ Reveals

BUDS ARE REVELATIONS

Now, in late March, pussy willows are budding all over the nation's northern tier of states. While most of Nature seems to be taking its last few winks of sleep under blankets of last autumn's leaves, the pussy willows, teased by March breezes, have wakened and stirred. Like spoiled children, who, when awake, will let no one else sleep, these fuzzy fellows now signal the North that spring is on its way, and every drowsy creature must be up, wide-awake and lively.

Spring-hungry city-dwellers now venture into the country-

side and probe along the wood's edge, the brook's bank and the margins of marshes for stands of willow shrubs, and gather twigs of pussy willows with dew-drops on their silvery, swollen catkins catching glints of spring sunshine and glistening like freshly polished jewels. Then, delighted with their find, the adventurers return home to put the willow twigs in vases and display them as sure signs that winter is receding and brighter, warmer days are just ahead.

A pussy willow is far more than a *mere* pussy willow. It is a revelation of something bigger than a budded branch. It says something significant about the entire earth, and brings joyous good news about the future.

Budding willows remind us of the earth's turning so that our hemisphere points sun-ward. They prompt us to remember that just now spring is surging through country swamp and meadow, through city lawns and parks, through every live trunk and branch and twig, through grass blade, crocus blossom and tulip shoot. Like transfused blood in a sick man's body, new life is racing through the arteries of the earth, bringing warmth to all things that, for months, have languished in coldness.

Pussy willows joyously proclaim "Spring is coming!" just when it seems winter will never end. The buds of these plants swell and burst as if with gladness that the secret of forth-coming springtime has been whispered to them by some gossiping breeze, and they cannot contain the happy tidings.

CHRIST REVEALS THE CHARACTER OF GOD

As spring advances and Lent draws to a close it is helpful to recall that as buds are revelations of something beyond themselves, reminding us not of themselves but of the advent of springtime, so Christ is more than a mere man seeking the world's attention and occupying space in history.

He is more than even a sublimely great man, or even the very greatest man of all time. He is more than a spiritual frontiersman, or the best of rabbis, or the saintliest of all saints, or the most heroic of all martyrs.

Jesus Christ is a *revelation* of God. Rather than pointing always to Himself, claiming attention for Himself, He points beyond Himself. He reveals the character of God. For millions of His followers He is the portrait of God fashioned from human flesh, the Almighty God reduced to your size and mine. As He Himself put it, "He that hath seen me hath seen the Father." (John 14:9). (This is one of the most awesome, staggering statements in all religious literature. Either Jesus was right, or he was deluded and insane, or a fraud.)

Jesus Christ shows us what we most need to know, what God is like. God is loving as Christ was loving, forgiving as Christ was forgiving, redemptive as Christ was redemptive. God cares

48

most for human welfare as human welfare counted most with Christ. Even God could do no better than to be like Christ.

CHRIST REVEALS PERFECT MANHOOD

Moreover, Christ is more than a revelation of God. He is the supreme revelation of what perfect *manhood* would be, if mortal man could achieve it. His moral excellency illumines the world.

When we are bewildered by conflicting moral standards and, amidst changing moral codes, we wonder what is worth preserving, we look to Him. Christ does not merely say, "You ought to do this," "You ought to put the welfare of others first," or "Your chief aim should be service." He *did* what man most needs to do; He put the welfare of others before His own welfare; He was the servant of all He met. He is, thus, not history's greatest theorist, but history's greatest *fact*, not a mere ideal, but an Event that has taken place in history. He did not so much preach the good life: He demonstrated it.

Jesus is thus this world's supreme and unique revelation of what life here should be like. Many would-be reformers of society miserably fail because they never present a working model of what a good man or good society should be like. Jesus, the Redeemer, was a working model of the God-controlled life. He illustrated it by a reverent sensitivity concerning what the will of God is and by a resolute determination to do God's will; by an abandonment of His own comforts and safety for the good of others; by a breaking of the wall men have erected between the sacred and the secular, between holy days and common days, so that ever after His coming it has been apparent that prayer and work alike are sacred, as are preaching and ploughing, altars and work benches.

When we obey this revelation of what life here should be like, and follow the clues He has given us, our lives become somewhat like His own. We then care less about success in terms of the world's loud acclaim and more about the faithful fulfillment of God's purposes. He was one of the poorest of men, who said, "The foxes have holes and the birds of the air have nests, but the Son of Man hath not where to lay his head." Nevertheless, He "went about doing good," enriching the lives of all He touched.

When we keep our attention focused on Him and His way

49

of life, our capacity to know God's will broadens and deepens. The God-dimension is added, so that we care less about the length of our years here and more about the *quality* of life spent here.

Jesus demonstrated a self-sacrificing love that reached across all races and religions, across all classes; a trust in the Heavenly Father's care that accompanied Him in sunshine and storm, when adoring crowds shouted, "Hosanna to the Son of David!" and when His infuriated enemies screamed, "Crucify Him!" He revealed a firm, unshakable certainty in God's final victory over evil, because this is His creation and subject at last to His sovereign will.

HOW TO DRAW LIFE'S TRUE DIMENSIONS

Like a child learning to draw from a model, and never taking more than a stroke or two with pencil or crayon without looking again at the model, so Christ's followers — at their best — have learned to draw life's true dimensions by looking frequently at Jesus, the Model of what the God-filled, God-ruled life is like.

In his autobiography, *The Unexpected Years*, Lawrence Housman related an incident which took place during a rehearsal of his stage play on the Nativity. Instructions called for the Wise Men to pay homage to the Holy Child and then retire from the stage. At that moment all lights were to be switched off, except for one light shining softly on the manger. But some stagehand clumsily turned off all the lights, leaving the entire stage in darkness. Then a voice rang out from backstage, "Here — you've switched off Jesus!"

The world can do no worse in these days of world crisis than to switch off Jesus. And it can do no better than to turn Him on. For He shows us what God is like, what God expects of us, and how man must conduct himself toward his fellowman if he is to survive.

13
The Tug of God

Simonides, an ancient Greek philosopher and poet who lived several centuries before Christ, was commanded by his king to offer a definition of God. The philosopher asked for a few moments to give the matter some thought. But so short a time did not suffice, and at the close of the day he returned to the palace and said, "O King, I shall require a week. I beg of you, grant me a week." At the week's end Simonides pleaded with the King for a month's time to define God. When the month was ended, the philosopher appeared before the monarch and asked for an extension of time: "I shall require a year, O King!" But before the year had ended, Simonides requested an audience with the King and confessed the task of defining God was quite beyond him: "O King, the more I think of God, the less I know of Him."

The wiser a man becomes, the more aware he is of his ignorance. Nowhere is this more true than in religion. The devout person is conscious of how little he knows about God and God's governance of the universe. This awareness of human limitation does not frighten or worry the reverent; instead it heightens his appreciation of his faith, for he knows that a God who could be completely understood would be inferior to man. (For is not man himself man's chief enigma?)

Arrogance is commonly associated with ignorance, and humility is the companion of knowledge and profound thought. A young woman was seated next to a famed astronomer at a public banquet. They introduced themselves to each other, but the pretty young thing did not recognize the astronomer's name. After the introductory remarks, the scientist asked, "What are you doing these days?" She answered that she was a junior at the university. "And what do you do?" inquired the girl. "I study astronomy," the distinguished man replied. "Oh, yes, astronomy! I finished that last year!" the girl said with a hint of condescension in her voice.

Too frequently we find a similar attitude in religion. The less some people think of God and experience God, the more certain they are that they know all there is worth knowing about Him. (Or the more convinced they are that religion is silly superstition or pure illusion.) To others, "a little knowledge is a dangerous thing," because it satisfies their mild interest and gratifies their small appetite. They feel that to give a little thought to religion is the same as mastering it. Too easily we believe that we know all that is worth knowing about God when we have read the Bible from cover to cover, when we have taken catechism classes, or when we have united with the church.

The Biblical injunction given through Moses, "Thou shalt not make unto thee any graven image or likeness . . ." was intended to disabuse man of the idea that he could ever capture the exact likeness of God in anything man could make, chiefly because man could never fathom the nature of God. While the Israelites' pagan neighbors worshiped images of earthly things, God's people understood that the Eternal was beyond man's sight, thought and grasp. No earthly symbol could ever encompass the meaning of God or even faintly hint at God's greatness.

Early Christianity was humble. It made no pretense of knowing much about God, and it made little attempt to explain or prove God. Rather, early Christians celebrated the mystery of God's nature and accentuated it by pointing to another mystery — the incomprehensible love of Christ, saying, "See, God is like that, beyond our imagination and fondest hope." At their best, Christians have always been humbly ignorant, gladly acknowledging the unintelligible, mysterious, transcendent nature of God. Instead of analyzing Him, arguing about Him or trying to prove Him, they have lived in His Presence in wonder, awe, and trust.

Critics of the life of faith have felt that this elusive quality of God's nature, the way God transcends our vision and our grasp, is the weak point in religion. Some have claimed that if the Supreme Power cannot be comprehended by our senses, there must be no God at all. Thus, Russian cosmonauts believed they had scored a point for atheism when they returned from their first long flight into space and reported that they had searched the heavens and found no God there. But, of course, this is no sound argument at all. One could examine the brain of a cosmonaut without finding a mind, or a thought, or an interest in space science. One could dissect a cosmonaut's heart and find no desire or courage for his task, and no love for wife or children or nation. Such an investigation of the heavens, or of brain, or heart proves nothing; for the most significant things in the universe are invisible. Space science, while using visible things, such as launching pads, booster rockets, space capsules, countless instruments and cosmonauts, is itself based upon the invisible. The yearning for space adventure is real, but no one has ever seen or weighed a yearning. Scientific knowledge and courage are real, but no one has ever measured an ounce of knowledge or a square foot of courage.

The most important things of earth and heaven are invisible. They are beyond the reach of our physical senses. But we do know of their effects. We see the tides and the moon that affects the tides, but the power that causes the vast bodies of earth's waters to respond to the moon's pull, no man has ever seen. We are aware that in March sap rises in trees, and in the northern parts of this continent we see men hanging buckets on maples to catch the amber sweetness. But the mysterious force that draws sap from roots of trees to the topmost twigs no one has ever seen.

A passer-by watched a lad flying a kite in the strong March breezes. The man traced the string until it disappeared behind heavy, low-lying clouds. Jokingly he said to the lad, "Son, I see your kite-string but no kite. Maybe you have no kite there at all!" "Oh yes, I have," the lad replied. "I can feel the tug of it!" God is a mystery beyond our sight. But God is real. We feel the power of His pull upon us. He tugs upon our souls when we witness the breath-taking beauty of creation spread lavishly around us, when we apprehend some fragment of truth that changes the direction of our lives, and when we see some sign of the Great Goodness in the sacrificial deeds of kindness of one of His children. And we see it supremely in the person of Jesus Christ, who is all of God that could be crammed into a body such as ours.

Summer Days

14

Stored Sunshine

Now, at the height of summer, drowsy cattle graze knee-deep in the lushness of sun-bleached meadows. Daisies splash pastures with bright yellow hues. Grain stalks hang heavy with golden seeds. Fruit bends the boughs of orchard trees. Gardens burst and overflow with flowering magic and ripe vegetables. And all of this rampant, burgeoning life is largely traceable to the sun's light and warmth.

The sun's rays fall so softly, silently and unobtrusively upon the earth that we are seldom aware of its beneficence. We easily forget that if the sun should not rise at its appointed time, within a few hours life would be extinct upon the earth. All living things, so the scientists tell us, are either directly or indirectly dependent upon the sun's radiance. Green plants capture and use in their growth the light and warmth of the heavens. Additional energies from above are saved in reserve within the tissues of plants. When we harvest vegetation from field, garden and orchard, we collect the stored sunshine of earlier days. Thus we benefit in August, in December or in frigid, bleak February from the sunshine of other hours.

Even the meat we eat is preserved sunlight. Cattle, pigs and sheep and fowl feed upon vegetation which, in turn, has fed upon the energy of the sun (and the nutrients in the soil). When you consume beef or pork or fish or fowl you are absorbing stored sunshine, "once removed."

Thus such words as "green corn" and "alfalfa hay," "wild strawberries," "carrots," "grapes," "apples," and "blueberries" are synonyms for sunshine held in reserve. And, because all creatures that devour vegetation, or that consume other creatures that are sustained by vegetation, depend upon the sun's vast energies, such words as "cattle," "sheep" and "pigs" and "robins," "bluebirds" and "woodthrush," and even "man" are prosaic ways of saying "stored sunshine."

The devout soul is engaged in a process similar to that of the growing plant. He is open and hospitable to Heaven, upon which he depends. He basks in the Light and absorbs it. "Thy

55

word have I hid in mine heart, that I might not sin against thee," said the Psalmist (Psalm 119:11). The Revised Standard Version more accurately uses the expression "laid up," signifying storage, rather than "hid." The Psalmist stored the most penetrating insights, the most essential truths and enduring wisdom he could acquire from the Holy Writings, public worship and every other encounter with the Eternal, knowing that in them strength could be found that would serve him well in days of testing. Then, on his *worst* days, he would benefit from his *best* hours and draw on reserves of stored sunshine.

Private prayer, like public worship and Bible reading, is one method of preserving one hour's power for another hour's need. Indeed, it is the most effective way. Even our Lord did not attempt to satisfy the spiritual and physical needs of the multitudes without first soaking up light and strength, spiritual resources that He later gave to others. He frequently stepped aside from the pressures of busy, hurried daily life and walked solitary ways, found a secluded place in the mountain, or at the desert's edge, or in a garden, and there exposed His spirit to an intense consciousness of the Father's greatness, goodness and purpose for Christ's life on earth. He went to his Source. Then, His spirit quickened and His energies recharged, He returned to the multitudes to perform His redemptive mission.

The first Christians learned from their Lord the effects of prayer. Their strength was found in being open to power from Beyond. Their secret of triumphant living was not in frantically trying harder than their neighbors, but in greater openness toward God. They could love others because they had first received Love, could be patient, forgiving and merciful, because patience, forgiveness and mercy had come to them from Above. They had basked in it, absorbed it, and — like grasses, grains and fruits that make their substance with the power of sunshine — the first Christians made a transformed daily life from the assimilated goodness of God.

56

A good memory is full of preserved light and warmth. Whenever we sacredly use our memories to review God's goodness to the people of Israel and to the Christian Church, whenever we employ memory to reflect upon God's great, saving love and power revealed through Jesus Christ and His kindness and mercy in our own individual experience we are drawing on rich inner reserves long ago stored away. A good memory is not one that possesses instant and complete recall of multitudes of facts. A truly "good" memory is full of *good things*. It is filled with the radiance of former golden hours. It overflows with stored sunshine, and thus brightens all our days.

Professor Sir Arthur Eddington, famed physicist of the University of Cambridge, once said, "The best absorbers are the best emitters." This is more than a law of the physical universe; it is the way the spiritual realm operates. We can give only after we have received.

Only those who have bathed in the illumination and warmth of Heaven and have transformed that exposure into energy of spirit are really prepared to serve the elemental spiritual needs of the world.

15

Spring-fed

The reason our stream keeps flowing through hot weather and drought, when water tables are generally low, and when many other brooklets have entirely evaporated, is that this brook has its source in inexhaustible springs. These natural fountains lie only half a mile to the east of us. From these sources happy streamlets skip toward each other, join, and then romp through open pasture and dense woods toward Lake Charlevoix, and on their way the capering waters pass through the forty acres known to us as Hidden Brook.

While driving over country roads some summer days, I have seen the parched, stony beds of vanished rivulets. Then fears for the welfare of our stream have plagued my mind until I could get to Hidden Brook. Always I have been gratified to find it there, sometimes running low, its tinkling laughter less gay, but never allowing its spirits to be entirely subdued. It is a dependable stream. It is spring-fed.

One reason for the anxiety and uncertainty of our times is that too many people are seeking satisfaction in streams that easily evaporate. They are counting on a perishable popularity, or impermanent health, or transitory wealth, and seeking gratification in passing pleasures while plagued with the haunting fear "Supposing something happens." We are easily dismayed by life's transitory na-

58

ture. Andre Gide once remarked that he had known a man who was plunged into darkest despair at the mere thought of having to replace the worn shoes he was wearing, or his clothing, linen, and necktie. His problem, Gide insisted, was not one of stinginess, but anguish at not being able to depend upon anything as being durable. He was tortured by a lack of absolutes.

Anyone who looks for an abundance of absolutes in this life is bound for disappointment. The newness and usefulness of shoes and clothes will fade. Some ideas, like "the inevitability of progress," are fashionable today and obsolete tomorrow. The playthings we clamor for at three years of age we regard as foolish at thirteen, and the "puppy love" of sixteen-year-olds is laughed at by sixty-year-olds who have forgotten the excitement of being "in love with love."

But, thank God, there are some spring-fed streams that do not run dry, and we need to find them. There are some homes that we can resort to, knowing that we will find there a dependable flow of love and concern — not gushing sentiment today and bone-dry indifference tomorrow.

There are spring-fed friendships where we, like thirsty deer coming to water, can always find refreshment allowing us to go back to our duties and our work mentally stimulated, reassured that life is good, our joys redoubled, our griefs somewhat assuaged, our sympathies broadened. Friends may come and go. We can lose friends, but we need not lose our capacity for friendship. Indeed, we dare not, for it is one of these streams that keep the soul alive.

There are churches that are spring fed, dependably inspiring and helpful, stemming from fountains of vitality and flowing with faith, profound insights, high hopes, noble purposes, and spiritual courage.

The kind of faith that makes for confidence in our tomorrows is the trust that when my present strength is spent more will be available. It comes from knowing that God is a source that never goes dry, that His grace is beyond the blight of drought, that His love is unending, and that His grace and love flow through the fields and forests of my being now and will as long as I live.

16
What's Your Hurry?

Some of the weed-killers now on the market kill noxious plants by stimulating the weeds' cells to greater activity than the weeds can tolerate. The plants then exhaust themselves by the excessive busyness of their cells, and they die. They are poisoned by busyness.

These days, when the tempo of life is moving faster and faster, we are in peril of destroying our souls by too much busyness. We move through our brief days so rapidly that the hours are blurred, and so are the highest values, such as family, friendship and worship. We hurry about trying to *do* so many things that we forget to feed our souls so that we can be worthwhile people.

Some anonymous waggish writer of verses once described a female do-gooder who spent her energies at a furious pace:

> *On Monday she lunched with a housing committee;*
> *With statistics and stew she was filled;*
> *Then she dashed to a tea on "Crime in Our City,"*
> *And dined with a Church Ladies Guild.*
>
> *On Tuesday she went to a Babies' Week Lunch*
> *And a tea on "Good Citizenship";*
> *At dinner she talked to the Trade Union bunch*
> *(There wasn't a date she dared skip).*
>
> *On Wednesday she managed two annual dinners,*
> *One at noon and the other at night,*
> *On Thursday a luncheon on "Bootlegging Sinners,"*
> *And a dinner on "War: Is It Right?"*
>
> *"World Problems We Face" was her Friday noon date,*
> *(A luncheon address, as you guessed),*
> *And she wielded a fork while a man from New York*
> *Spoke that evening on "Social Unrest."*

On Saturday noon she fell in a swoon,
Missed a talk on the youth of our land. . . .
Poor thing, she was through! She never came to,
But died with a spoon in her hand.

Such small souls are easily poisoned by their busyness. Moreover, they also hurt others, depriving them of the companionship they need. One father, reciting the hard luck he and his wife had suffered, said to a friend, "We lost our first child." The friend, shocked, exclaimed, "I didn't know your daughter was dead!" "Oh, she isn't dead," the father responded. "I was just too busy."

There are some people near to every one of us, and children are among them, who are disappointed, depressed, defeated, embittered, bored, weary, anxious and frightened, lonely, rejected, blighted by their own sins and hurt by man's inhumanity to man. They need some word of cheer you can speak, some thoughtful deed you can perform. Are you too busy to notice? Too busy to act? What are you doing that is so much more important than their need?

Soon after a certain business man died, his family erected a tombstone over his grave with an epitaph reading, "Born a human being. Died a wholesale grocer." Busyness can dehumanize us, poison and wither our souls, and keep us so excessively preoccupied making a living that we forget how to live.

We pass through this world but once. Why rush past the scenery? Why miss the slow savoring of friendships, the beauty of nature? Why overlook the skills of our fellows, their artistry in painting, sculpture, architecture, music and literature? Why miss the good we can do, the kindnesses we can show?

Why miss the goodness of God, which is apparent only to those who *take time to count life's blessings?*

What's your hurry?

17

What to Do About Interruptions

An exclamation commonly heard around our homes, shops, offices and golf courses is "Don't interrupt me!" We all suffer interruptions. Is there anyone, anywhere, who really enjoys them?

An eight-year-old Philadelphia lad has made a sign that he hangs on the door of his room when he secludes himself. The sign reads, "DO NOT ENTER WITHOUT KNOCKING. DO NOT EVEN KNOCK." We sympathize with his mood. It is often ours, too.

A teacher, testing whether his physics students had studied their lesson on specific gravity, asked, "What happens when a body is immersed in water?" One observing lad answered, "The telephone rings!" That response is true to life. Start to take a bath and the telephone rings. Become interested in a radio or television program and someone switches the set to another station. Plan a quiet weekend of rest at home, and a houseful of company arrives unannounced. Begin preparations for a profession and the armed forces demand your services, or money runs out, or suddenly marriage seems more important, and you marry instead. Plan to continue your education in spite of marriage, and the babies start arriving. Decide to retire early from your business, and financial reverses intrude. "There's always something!"

William Coleridge's poem "Kubla Khan" was never finished. The poet himself could not say how it would have ended because of an annoying interference. Someone knocked at Coleridge's door. When the poet opened the door to let his visitor in, the idea of the poem fled and never returned.

I look outside my study windows at the grove of graceful birches that shade our brook, and I see that each tree is a little taller than last autumn, a trifle whiter, and the entire grove appears to be a bit lovelier, in spite of the interruption in their growth that a severe winter imposed. They glory and luxuriate in June, without sulking in wilted disgust over winter's thoughtless interference.

What do you do about your interruptions? Resent them?

Become bitter about them? Do you simply shrug your shoulders in helpless resignation and say, "Well, that's the way life is!"? Or do you make a creative use of life's interferences?

There is an art in handling interruptions. See what Jesus did with them. His redemptive manner of living enabled Him to recognize in His interruptions splendid opportunities for doing good. When mothers brought infants to Jesus for the blessings of His attention and touch, the disciples resented the interference. Jesus had no time for little children; only grownups deserved His time and concern, so the disciples thought. This interruption Jesus used to teach all who would listen that the directness, openness, trustfulness and unsophisticated simplicity of little children are required spiritual traits of all who belong to God: "Let children come to me. Do not prevent them. The Kingdom of God belongs to the childlike."

When a religious leader interrupted Jesus while He was giving comfort and healing to the sick, and denounced the Master for healing a terribly crippled, utterly wretched person on the Sabbath, Jesus used the occasion to show that human need rather than narrow ecclesiastical ordinances should have priority in the minds of God's people.

Jesus' periods of solitude and prayer were rudely violated by the clamor of the crowds and by the cry of His friends, "Everyone is looking for you!" Far from being irritated or angry, the Master responded to such interference with understanding and compassion. He was needed. There was something He could do, some light He could shed in darkness, some disease of soul or body He could heal, some word from God He would speak. Don Herold has said, "Interruptions are the spice of life." They *can* give life a higher flavor. When frustrating hindrances broke into the Master's plans, He converted those vexations into victories, all obstructions into opportunities, all stumbling blocks into stepping stones.

Much as Columbus, hoping to reach India by sailing westward, bumped into undiscovered America instead, so Christ's unsought interruptions became new worlds of adventure in teaching and redemption.

May all of your obstructions become opportunities.

18

Self-Expression Is Not Enough

One sunny afternoon some years ago a fellow townsman guided me on a walk over a farm he had inherited from his sister several years earlier. Since the land had cost the man no back-bending labor and sweat, since nothing of himself was invested in the farm, he had placed little value upon the acreage. He had ploughed no fields, planted no crops, harvested no grain, mended no fences. The fields were waist-high in burdock, thistles and all manner of other weeds. Where cows once plodded to pasture after sunrise milking time and homeward again at sunset, the lanes were choked with rank growths of noxious plants. Brambles infested fence rows and overran the old orchard.

That was a farm emancipated from man's interference, and every square yard bore witness to the land's self-government. It was literally a "land of liberty," a real utopia of independence and self-expression. And it was ugly to see.

Now, years later, when someone speaks to me of the glories of free self-expression, I think of that abandoned farm. It was unrepressed by plough, cultivator or hoe. It was unbiased by the sowing of any particular seed by the hand of man, and it could grow what it pleased. It pleased to grow weeds.

Our twentieth century culture has elevated self-expression to a ridiculously high place among the virtues. "Don't fence me in" has become our motto for personal behavior. The gospel shouted by the expressionists advises us to let ourselves go. Discard restricting moral codes. Be yourself. Let liberty become libertinism.

Self-expression has become the god of the fine arts. Cast aside all standards in painting, sculpture, poetry and music. Slap on the paint. Throw the clay together any way it happens to clot. Toss words in abstract heaps and call them "poetry." Bang the drums. Thump the piano. Squeal on the clarinet. Express yourself in sound. That is music!

One thing the cults of self-expression have forgotten is the importance of having *something to express*. They are more absorbed in being "characters" than in developing character; more fascinated by painting techniques than in subject matter; more interested in spouting verse than in possessing a meaningful, provocative thought that merits poetry; more concerned with making sound with instruments than in sensing some worthwhile message that music could ennoble and convey. Expressionists are determined to be heard, but give little thought as to what deserves being said.

Self-expression is not enough. In fact, raw self-expression is one of the most irritating influences we ever experience. What makes a bore a bore? One thing mainly, unrestrained self-expression. Whether he is conversing with an acquaintance or speaking to hundreds of listeners, the bore is hardly thinking of his audience at all. He speaks to relieve himself, and not to inform or inspire his hearers. Self-expression also characterizes the hypochondriac whose greatest pleasure is in locating and describing in great detail his vagrant aches and pains, as if the world were breathlessly awaiting the latest report. Such people are basically disinterested in others, excepting as others can serve their self-indulgence and let them have free rein for self-expression.

Is self-expression an evil thing, then? Not at all, providing there is within a person something worth expressing. While the abandoned farm, growing weeds, is self-expressive, so is the fruitful farm with its generous fields yielding tall corn, row on row, pumpkins on the vine, fruit hanging from every orchard bough and bins heaped with grain. The worst and best farms are alike in this: they are all self-expressive.

The criminal who stabs a man in a holdup is expressing himself, but so is the skillful, dedicated surgeon who saves the victim's life.

The gossip who attempts to debase her neighbors with the worst rumors about them is self-expressive, but so is the cheerful, kindly soul who inspires with words of hope and encouragement.

The brawler in the streets is expressing himself, but so is the high-minded civil servant battling corruption in government and struggling with social injustice.

The real value and significance of self-expression is in having within you something worth revealing to the world. The secret of the world's great achievers has been that of expressing

65

through themselves something *bigger* than themselves. The musician and painter reveal a beauty of sound, symmetry, line and color that were here on earth long before the musician and painter arrived and will remain long after they are gone. The scientist does not make truth. He reveals it. Truth was here before his birth, and truth will outlast him. He does not manufacture truth; he expresses it.

It is significant for every Christian that Jesus Christ, who has given us the clearest picture of God, said, "My teaching is not mine, but His that sent me." Even He could express only what He first received. He could make God real to men only by daily living in the presence of the Eternal.

The secret of significant self-expression is in having something to express.

In the words of an old benediction,

> Now may God be in your lips, and in all your speaking.
> May God be in your mind, and in all your thinking.
> May God be in your heart, and in all your living.

19

The World's Worst Curse Word

In my lifetime I have heard a great deal of ear-blistering profanity. During summer vacations in my boyhood I sometimes worked with a circus crew, putting up tents, bleachers and other equipment. It was a tough gang, and mistakes and minor accidents led to outbursts of cursing that severely shocked me at first, since I came from a home where profanity was never heard. Also, in those days I frequently visited the farm homes of relatives and friends, and when a cow kicked over a bucket of milk, or a ram butted a farmer carrying a basket of eggs, the creature was sometimes rebuked with withering blasphemy.

Like you, I am still exposed to the frustration, anger and outrage of men and hear their crude irreverence profanely spoken. But the most profane word I've ever heard is usually regarded to be but an innocent expression and not at all blasphemous. *The word is "hopeless."* It is profane because of what it implies. It represents an attitude defiled by futility and polluted with a Godless pessimism. It is a God-denying word. "Hopeless" means "Godless," for only a person, a situation or a world without God can be without hope.

The Christian never sees the world as hopeless because he cannot believe the world is Godless. The person of faith is aware of the God who has worked throughout history, whose power and influence are manifested in the creation of the universe, in sustaining the world, in freeing Hebrews from Egyptian bondage, in the moral guidance of the Ten Commandments, in speaking through prophets and poets. The man of faith knows the God revealed in Jesus Christ whom Herod's hordes failed to destroy when He was but a babe. He remembers that event that some must have thought hopeless — a cruel cross between two other crosses on a lonely hill and the dead Man nailed there.

The Christian recalls that three days after Christ died His tomb was empty and He was alive among His disciples and so real that He shattered their despair and replaced it with an unfailing faith that nothing is too hard for God. Christians are

67

conscious, too, of the history of the Church, beginning with what men thought to be a "hopeless" little band of disciples, struggling against persecution on all sides, pitted against the power of Rome, and in spite of the odds against it spreading throughout the world. So the Christian lives in hope because he is ever aware of God's victories in the past and dares to believe these triumphs portend God's final conquest of evil. It is a simple logic, mixed with faith: what God has done, God can still do.

Hopelessness means forgetting God's action in history. It means remaining emotionally in Egyptian bondage long after God's children have been freed. Hopelessness means living on the wrong side of Easter.

Hope is the confident trust that God still has good plans for us, and He is capable of realizing them. Such a faith brings order out of chaotic living, holds life together and is a preventive against mental and spiritual shiftlessness.

Several years ago a small town in Maine was condemned to drowning. A great hydro-electric plant was proposed for the area and this development meant a dam would be built across a nearby river. The waters would rise, submerging the town, which was located upstream from the dam site. When the project was announced the villagers were given many months to arrange their affairs and prepare to move.

In the interval, before work on the dam was started, a revealing situation developed in the town. All improvements ceased. No painting was done. No repairs were made on the buildings, the roads or sidewalks. Day after day the town grew shabbier. Long before the dam was built and the waters rose or the people moved away the town looked uncared for and abandoned. One citizen explained, "Where there is no faith in the future, there is no power in the present." The town was cursed! It was "hopeless."

Every generation and every soul needs hope if it is to avoid moral shabbiness. This distressed world needs it. Christian hope is the assurance that God has not abandoned us. It is the faith that a loving God has all the universe and our own private destinies in His capable hands, and He will, in His own good time, work out His wondrous plans with them.

Such a faith in the future puts power into everyday living.

20
The Junk Yard and the Park

Some years ago, in one of our southeastern states, a streetcar motorman found he had eleven minutes between his arrival at the end of his run and the time he was scheduled to start back over his route. At this stopping point there was a plot of land nobody cared about. The neglected piece of ground was perhaps one-half acre in size. Careless people had thrown old bottles and discarded tin cans there. Every vagrant wind blew wrappings and newspapers across the plot.

One day the motorman decided to use his leisurely eleven minutes at the end of each run to pick up loose papers. After several stops the land looked a little less littered. Then he began gathering tin cans and bottles, and on his day off he hauled them to the city dump. When spring came, he brought flower seeds, shrub cuttings and sapling trees, and at nearly every stop he sowed some seeds or planted some cuttings or young trees. With this program of using a little time every day the motorman converted the dumping ground to a small park that delighted the eye of everyone who passed.

A junk yard and a park symbolize two contrasting kinds of living, jumbled and purposeful. The junk yard's ugliness is found chiefly in its disorder. The stuff that is there may be old and broken, but its ugliness is not in its age or disrepair, for the goods in an antique shop are old and yet often beautiful, and material stacked neatly in a repair shop may be broken without being unsightly. More than any other feature, it is the disorderliness of a junk yard that makes it ugly.

A park is a planned place. There is a plot for grassy lawns, a spot for trees to grow, for streams or pools of water. Benches are there to sit on. There are walkways and places where walking is forbidden. In short, at opposite poles of our judgment of ugliness and beauty are the junk yard and its distasteful disorder and the park with its well-ordered loveliness.

From this we gather what beauty means in the realm of the spirit. The good and beautiful life is organized and controlled by high purpose, and not cluttered by ungoverned impulses.

We all have impulses, good and bad. Maturing into manhood and womanhood means developing principles of conduct that rule us instead of wild, disordered impulses. Growing up is, in part, a process of substituting plan and principle for impulse and mood. The infant is a package of impulses always spilling out all over anyone who is near. He cries, wets and sleeps when the impulse seizes him, and will do virtually nothing unless he is in the appropriate mood. But gradually, as he matures, the child learns to substitute principle for impulse. How many of us would have received an education if we had gone to school only on those days when we were enthusiastic about schooling? How many would have any credit standing if we paid bills only when we could do so cheerfully, gladly? How many would have a job if we reported for work only when we were eager for it and excited about it? How would government fare if only those voted who were fanatically patriotic? Would religious faith survive in the world if only those who were caught up in religious ecstasy went to church and were loyal to the Kingdom of God?

All good people everywhere have learned to live above mere wishes and whims. They live responsibly. Impulsiveness is a junk yard kind of living, where desires, moods, and whims are scattered helter-skelter and dominate the scenery. Purposive living is park-like living, where high principles and plan draw all of life's components into a great design.

The Christian knows what real goodness is, for he has seen it revealed in Jesus Christ. Christlikeness, then, is our goal, and Christ's own conduct is our standard.

Moreover, every park has a place for wild and unwanted things. There is a place for wild flowers as well as for cultivated plants. Insects and warty toads will be there. Somewhere handy the visitor will find waste baskets and trash cans for discarded litter and junk. The good life, too, must provide a place for unwanted things, the uncultivated, the wild, the pestiferous. Not everything in a garden or a life is wanted, but some things undesired must be accepted. We should make room in our thinking for criticism as well as praise, since no one of us is perfect, since all of us can improve, and since even the perfect person would be misunderstood and censored, as Jesus was.

There must be a place for drudgery as well as play, for failure as well as success, for difficulty as well as ease, for handicap and natural limitation as well as skill, for illness and pain as well as health, for grief as well as joy. Some of these we will accept and make room for in our lives, like wild growth in a garden, and others we will discard like waste paper in a trash basket. But the man of faith will not fretfully kick against life's occasional unpleasantness or become resentful and bitter. He will so order his life that there will be room for a few unwanted things.

The famed English author, Rudyard Kipling, and William Booth, founder of the Salvation Army, one day met at Oxford University. It was an occasion when honorary degrees were being conferred upon them. Old William Booth was not embarrassed in the slightest by being on the same platform with the highly literate Kipling. Booth marched across the quadrangle and asked Kipling, "Young feller, how's your soul?" Although crudely put, that is life's perennial and preeminent question, "What are you really like inside?" Beneath our veneer of worldly success and honors, beneath all appearances, what are we?

Junk yards?

Parks?

21

Sharing the Sunlight

Take a common weed in your hands. Twist it between your fingers, turning it about. Count the revolutions the stem must make before a leaf projects directly above the leaf where you began your count.

Leaves do not grow in random fashion upon a stem. They spring from their supporting stem in such a way as to give each other an equal amount of light. It would almost seem as if the Creator has blessed even the most common leaf on a roadside weed with a kindly consideration for all the other leaves on that plant, since each one is so positioned as to give every other one its share of sunshine.

One of the most important things that can happen to a person occurs when his interests grow outward toward other people, so that he recognizes their needs, desires and rights, and wants them to have their share of life's good things. We begin life as self-centered creatures. The things that interest us then are those that directly serve our elemental needs — the mother who nurses us, the bottle that pacifies us, the toy rattle that entertains us.

The emotional growth of some people is stunted at this stage. They remain forever self-indulgent, too much absorbed in self to see the beauty of the world, the dignity of human life or to think about the greatness and goodness of God. They are insistent upon the recognition of their own needs and rights and neglectful of the needs and rights of others. They are less likely to serve the people around them than to exploit them. Whenever such people declare, "I love you" they really mean, "I love *me,* and want you to make me happy." And they cannot even appreciate the love and consideration that parents, spouses and friends lavish upon them, for such devotion is accepted as a matter of course. It is due them.

One of the first lessons a child must be taught (and no one is truly adult, no matter his age, until he learns this lesson) is that he must adjust to the fact that there are others in his environment who have needs and desires that are just as real and just as urgent as his own. Therefore, he cannot take whatever he wishes, because others have wants as emphatic as his own. He cannot do or say whatever he pleases because others have feelings as sensitive as his own. The person who grows emotionally and spiritually becomes more and more conscious of others and their needs. He tries to keep himself out of their way, so that they can get their share of the sunlight.

Moreover, as we grow toward spiritual maturity we become more aware of how much others have contributed to our welfare. We are carried out of ourselves, beyond egotism, so that we acknowledge that other lives have been blended with ours, enriching us. Marian Anderson, the great Negro contralto, usually uses the impersonal "we" instead of "I" in her conversation. This gives her speech a touch of formality that some have found objectionable. During a trip to Asia a Buddhist scholar questioned her about this habit. Marian Anderson replied, "One realizes, the longer one lives, that there is no particular thing that one can do alone. Many people are involved in the work we do — those who wrote the music, those who made the pianos on which the accompanist plays, the accompanist who actually lends support to the performance. To go out without any of these things, to stand on your own — even the voice, the breath, the everything . . . it is not your doing. So the 'I' in it is very small, after all."

Yes, in the good life the "I" is very small. When we are at our best we know that God is big, and we are grateful for His light falling upon us. We restrain ourselves from overshadowing others who should get their share of Heaven's blessings. And we rejoice in all of those who have not selfishly absorbed all they could of life's richness, but have passed God's goodness our way.

Part 2

Holidays and Other Special Days

Autumn Holidays

22

The Meaning of Appreciation

One of the fairest spirits ever to grace America was Alice Freeman Palmer, professor of history at Wellesley College, and later president of that school. After she was already a noted educator she became the wife of the famed Greek scholar, philosopher and professor of religion at Harvard University, George Herbert Palmer. In his book *The Life of Alice Freeman Palmer,* Dr. Palmer told of the club Mrs. Palmer organized for little girls in one of Boston's dreariest slums. Called "The Happiness Club," the group had few rules, but one of them was that each child must see something beautiful each day.

That assignment might be easy for one whose home overlooked San Francisco Bay, or the valley of Yosemite, and it would not be too difficult for one who lived in a penthouse apartment overlooking Central Park in New York City. But in the drab streets and dingy alleyways of Boston's squalid tenement district that rule called for earnest searching and a lively imagination. Nevertheless, most of the girls mastered the art of finding something beautiful in their environment every day to report at their club meetings: the iridescent, rainbow colors shining from a strutting pigeon's neck and breast; raindrops dimpling the small puddles that formed on cobblestone streets; a vivid green blade of grass bravely forcing itself toward the sunlight from a crack in broken sidewalk.

Mrs. Palmer was not encouraging children to be content with their miserable lot. But she was developing within them an awareness of the beauty to be found everywhere by alert eyes and hospitable minds and hearts. She hoped they would make one of life's most joyous discoveries, that it is not how much we have but how much we appreciate that really makes for happiness.

There is much ugliness in the world, much dirt, sordidness and greed. Any idiot can find it, and any cynic can look upon it and say, "That's life!" But beauty is here, too, in small scattered particles in slums, in greater abundance among the mountains, in the forests, by the lakeside and ocean beach. But there is less difference in scenery than there is between seers.

The perception of beauty is not so much a matter of one's position as it is of one's disposition. And the proper disposition is one of appreciativeness.

What would the world of painting, sculpture, architecture, music, poetry and other literature be like if there were only creators but no appreciators? There would be artists, but no buyers or art museums, no listeners to music except the musicians, no readers except the writers. Without the fine art of appreciation all the other arts would be virtually lost.

Without appreciation there could be no religion, for religion is not mainly the mere knowledge that God exists, but appreciation of His handiwork, His Presence and His Goodness. Such appreciation means walking gently through God's world as a good guest walks through his host's house, careful not to hurt or deface what is God's — either His furnishings or His children.

In Scotland a botanist was examining a common heather bell under a microscope when a curious old shepherd approached the scientist, hopeful of discovering what had caught the botanist's fancy. The shepherd was allowed to look through the microscope at the simple flower. After a long, breathless pause the old fellow raised his head and exclaimed, "Mon, I wish ye had never shown it to me! I have trodden on so many of those lovely things."

Appreciation means stretching our rare moments of awe and reverence from an occasional encounter with exciting beauty to an awareness of all the minor beauties the Almighty has lavishly squandered at our feet. It means encouraging our minds to dwell on *all* the wonders we can find in God's world and letting the soul feast on what is commonplace, fundamental and lasting.

Appreciation is letting the mind review what we have already, rather than what we lack. It is reflection upon the two or three spiritual goods, the two or three people and the two or three material things that mean most to us, and then fancying how strenuously we would seek them if we lacked them.

Appreciation is gratitude converted into action. It is being so thankful for the good that has come our way that we want to pass it on to others. It is thanking God by helping our fellowmen. If we have strength, appreciation means helping the weak. If we have faith in God, it means encouraging the discouraged and cheering the hopeless. If we have enough food and clothing to keep us alive, it means giving to those on the thin edge of starvation and nakedness.

Appreciation is the ability to recognize and be grateful for talents that we do not possess, rather than to be envious of those who do have them. At a discussion of works of literature, a highly appreciative paper was read on the poetry of Percy Bysshe Shelley. While the paper was being discussed one member of the group said rather testily that he could see nothing of value in Shelley's poetry. The reader of the paper responded, "Mr. So-and-So says he does not see anything in Shelley. Poor devil!" The unappreciative are the world's "poor devils" — abjectly and permanently poor, for no matter what beauty, truth and goodness they may be exposed to, their souls absorb no richness.

The appreciative person is always rich, for he owns not only what he personally possesses, but his gratitude lays thankful claim on all the good that he surveys.

23

We Live by Our Appreciations

Before the Pilgrims sailed for America on the *Mayflower*, one of their number, Robert Cushman, wrote a disturbing letter to a friend. The outlook for their venture was bleak, he said. "If we ever make a plantation in the new world, God works a miracle! Specially considering how scant we shall be in victuals, and most of all ununited amongst ourselves. If I should write you of all the things which promiscuously forerun our ruin, I should overcharge my weak head and grieve your tender heart. Only this I pray you: prepare for evil tidings of us every day. Pray for us instantly. I see not, in reason, how we shall escape."

Cushman's worst fears were realized. During the first treacherous winter the Pilgrims spent in America food was so scarce that each Pilgrim was allotted a daily ration of five grains of corn. Even at the first Thanksgiving feast, the Pilgrims celebrated *meager* blessings — the survival of only about half of those who had landed at Plymouth, the construction of eleven crude shelters, a twenty-acre crop of Indian corn, a poor crop of barley, and peas that were not worth harvesting. When neighboring Indians appeared as guests for Thanksgiving meals, there was not enough food to serve them, so the Indians left Plymouth Colony to hunt deer. They returned with fresh venison, and the celebration proceeded.

Three thousand miles of wild ocean stretched between the

Pilgrims and the comforts they had left behind in Europe. But in these miserable circumstances self-pity and whining complaint were total strangers. These pioneers were poor in material goods but rich in appreciation. They reflected upon their present blessings, of which they had only a few, rather than upon their past misfortunes, of which there were many. And they gave thanks.

Although Thanksgiving Day is now officially proclaimed by the chief of government, any Thanksgiving worthy of the name arises from a spirit of appreciation in the people, and not from presidential proclamations. (The word "appreciate" comes from a Latin origin meaning "to prize." The appreciator is a person sensitive to the values of what he sees and possesses.) Thanksgiving Day is celebrated, not because God needs our praise to boost a sagging ego, and not because when we give thanks we reveal to God a commendable inner attitude He might not have guessed we possessed. Instead, we celebrate Thanksgiving because we need an occasional reminder of something we so easily forget: *we live by our appreciations.*

When we concentrate on the good things that have happened to us, as the Pilgrims did, rather than complain about our discontents, our spirits thrive and grow. When we take God's goodness for granted and casually accept the kindnesses of our fellowmen without gratitude, we suffocate our souls. The Pilgrims lived vitally, not because their situation was ideal, for it wasn't, but because they were appreciative of the good to be found in even the worst circumstances. This truth is so simple and commonplace that we overlook it. Nevertheless it is the truth of which Thanksgiving Days are made.

Why is it that we pay less attention to our everyday blessings than to our occasional great losses? Isn't this because of deficient appreciation? The parents of a boy killed in the war presented their church with a substantial gift to be used for a suitable memorial for their son. The mother of another soldier learned of the gift and suggested to her husband that they also make a contribution. The husband protested, "Why should we? Our son came home from the war." "That is precisely the point," the mother said. "Let's make a gift of thanksgiving because he did come home!" What a difference we could make in the world if we would spend as freely in recognition of our joys as we do in solemn memorial of our losses!

Can you imagine your happy surprise at seeing notices in the newspapers that ring a glorious change on the obituaries? "Yesterday Fred Johnson returned home from the hospital and is convalescent from a tumor operation. In joyful memory of this occasion friends are invited to join his grateful family in contributing to the American Cancer Society." Or "Rebecca Jones is recovering from her recent critical heart attack. Her family and friends, who were fearful they would be attending her funeral, are now showering her with affection and care. If you wish to join in our joy, give to the American Heart Association." Or "The Joseph Jacksons rejoice in announcing the birth of a son, Joseph Jr., weight seven pounds, three ounces. He is healthy and certain to be a future President. Friends who wish to share our happiness may give to the Retarded Children's Center or to the Foundling Fund of Children's Hospital." Wouldn't all our lives be richer and all the world happier if we would be as careful to memorialize our blessings as we do our losses?

The Pilgrims did. That is how we got Thanksgiving Day.

24

Thank God for Rare Blessings

God's rare gifts have a special charm. The flowers that interest us most are those that cannot be seen just any time one has the desire. They are here only occasionally, and one must be alert for the occasion when they burst into bloom with brisk urgency, or they will be missed entirely. Seasonal flowers such as yellow or pink lady slippers, columbine and twin-flowers, wood lilies and golden asters and countless others curtsy to the seasons, linger briefly and bow out, not to be seen again until their special season returns. It is their transiency that gives them their special charm.

One reason whitetail deer in a public park seem comparatively dull is that we know they are always there, to be seen any time we look. So they lose our interest. But wild deer are elusive and appear unpredictably, walking, unconcerned, near a cabin beneath the pines, standing statue-still and silhouetted against the translucent light of a misty dawn, or daintily sipping from our favorite fishing hole in the brook. Deer are not so often watched as they are merely glimpsed. They surprise us with their appearance; therein is their charm.

Some of the best things in life are appreciated most when caught only in glimpses. When they are constantly ours, they lose much of their attractiveness. Rest is good in small doses, but wearisome when it must be continued for weeks or months. Humor is a delight in small amounts sprinkled lightly through conversation or public speech. But a constant, prolonged flow of jesting is monotonous and exhausting. An occasional word of praise is appreciated by everyone, but protracted applause becomes boresome. Occasional moments of ecstatic joy add relish to life, but there is no such thing to be found on earth as perpetual happiness. When pleasure is unrelieved by inconvenience, adversity, disappointment or struggle, it turns into tedious humdrum.

The most exciting things lose their attraction when made perpetual. Sports do. Imagine being compelled to spend ten hours a day, six days a week, and fifty-two weeks out of every year watching baseball or football games or playing golf or tennis. Soon a sport becomes hard work rather than recreation if watched or engaged in constantly. A sport has its greatest value when it represents change from life's routine and when it is engaged in only occasionally.

An occasional smile charms us, but a smile that never leaves is found only on the faces of blithering idiots.

The conversationalist who alternates his talk with eager listening fascinates us. If a person constantly chatters he repels us. Good conversation is a mixture of occasional talk, occasional listening and occasional silence.

Here is one sound secret of joyous living: refuse to take for granted the good God has given you. Use your imagination. Pretend that the blessings that come your way regularly are really scarce.

1. Deal with members of your family with the courtesy you show near-strangers. Greet your own child with the politeness, interest and admiration you show to your employer's dimple-

cheeked, curly-haired little boy. Speak to your spouse with the gentleness and respect you reserve for the pretty clerk at the drugstore or the vice-president in charge of loans at the bank. Be as thoughtful to your marriage partner as you were in the days of your courtship.

2. Look upon every starlit night as if stars appeared but once in a lifetime, at the moon as if it were but a onetime visitor to our solar system, at a tree as if it were the first and last tree God had planted upon earth.

3. Use your eyes today as if you had been blind all your days and as if after midnight tonight you would return to perpetual darkness. Look at God's world and God's children, at strangers and at your loved ones, as if this were your only day for seeing.

4. Appreciate one hour of health as if it were the only painless hour you would ever know.

5. Pray as if you had just now heard for the first time about the goodness and greatness of God and as if this were your only opportunity to talk to God or to listen to Him. Pray the Lord's Prayer just once in that fashion, instead of from easy memory, and see the difference it makes in your comprehension of its meaning.

Man sins more from boredom than from lust. Man's thanklessness comes less from greed than from taking the goodness of God and man for granted.

Restore adventure, excitement and gratitude to everyday life by treating common blessings as great occasions.

Winter Holidays

25

Remember Bethlehem

How can God possibly be concerned with individuals? His universe is so vast and we are so small. You are but one person among billions of people, and the earth on which billions of your kind dwell is but one negligible planet among billions of heavenly bodies. The scientists invite us to suppose that the earth could be reduced to the size of the period at the end of this sentence, the diameter of which is about one-fiftieth of an inch. Imagine that everything else in the universe were reduced proportionately. On that microscopic scale, with the earth the size of a period, the sun would be only 19½ feet from the earth. The nearest star would be 1,005 miles away, and the farthest known galaxy of stars would be nearly 82 billion miles away. Such would be the size of the universe if the earth were a little more than pin-point size. Mighty vast, isn't it?

To many people a universe of such boundless spaces and staggering distances is frightening and bewildering. They would find it far easier to have faith in God's personal interest in them if the world were small and cozy. The fathomless depths of space make the Creator seem far-off and impersonal. How could God care for one human being when He has such a creation to supervise?

While we rejoice in the immensities that stretch our thoughts, and glory in the beauty, symmetry, orderliness and power that reveal to us something of the Creator's might and skill, such an awesome picture of creation leaves us dissatisfied because we still know so little about the Creator's heart. God is mighty, but is He interested in people like you and me? God is great, but is God tender and loving? The physical universe tells us something about the Creator, just as a painting by Leonardo da Vinci tells us something about that artist's sense of draftsmanship, perspective, feeling for composition and color. But a painting leaves us dissatisfied as to the character of the artist,

whether he was cowardly or courageous, stingy or generous, mean or kind. So, our picture of the universe tells us much less about God's nature than we need to know. While we are awestruck by what God has done, we crave to know what kind of God did it.

Then we turn to another world that reveals something of the character of God. It is that little world, within a big world, the village of Bethlehem and its cattle stall. The Gospel of Saint Luke tells of an angel joyously anouncing to fear-smitten shepherds, "Fear not; for behold, I bring you good tidings of great joy, which shall be to all people. For unto you is born this day in the city of David a Saviour, which is Christ the Lord. And this shall be a sign unto you; ye shall find the babe wrapped in swaddling clothes, lying in a manger." At the manger of Bethlehem we see God revealed as self-giving, as gentleness and as a love that we cannot find in the farthest outstretches of the Milky Way nor discover in the infinite spread of galaxies that dwarf the one in which our universe is set.

The Babe of Bethlehem did for us what astronomy cannot: He showed us the character of God. He grew to love supremely well, to be gentle when hardness and retaliation seemed called for. He was concerned for others when they were self-serving and negligent of Him.

Since no stream can rise higher than its source, and nothing God has made can be better than the God who made it, we know that God must be as good as Christ. So the early Church proclaimed Christ's birth as glorious good news. At last believers in God could announce with glad certainty what God was like. They said that in spite of God's awful might and lofty goodness, far above anything man could know or be, God is concerned about individuals here on earth. "The Word became flesh and dwelt among us." What is God like? "God is Christlike," they sang. The world is governed by the Lord of Love.

And ever since the Babe of Bethlehem completed His mission on earth, the core of Christian faith has *not* been the belief that God exists, but that a loving God *lives among us*. That is the meaning of Bethlehem.

When life is drab, commonplace and unpromising, remember Bethlehem. In your dullest, most ordinary and most monotonous moment, God is as near you as He was to the dingy, lack-luster, gray-brownish huts of sun-baked clay set along the narrow, cramped, unpleasant-smelling streets of that unspectacular little town of Bethlehem where nothing important ever happened. But life brightened on that far-off night for those who knew that God had come among them.

Is anything in the world irredeemably dull or commonplace if God can bathe Bethlehem's streets with starlight and touch a manger with sudden glory and make of baby-flesh such a Savior?

Christmas points to the exciting, divine possibilities of any life when God comes into it. Remember Bethlehem.

When loneliness torments you, remember Bethlehem. When God seems far away and disinterested in your woes and griefs, your problems and perplexities, remember the manger and the Holy Family.

Joseph and Mary on that first Christmas night were alone in a place of crowds; and there is no greater loneliness than that felt in a throng of strangers, as any little child separated from his parents and lost in a mob of Christmas shoppers can tell you. Apparently they had no relatives in Bethlehem, or they would have sought shelter with them. They received no invitations to go anywhere. Socially they were "left out." At last an innkeeper let them stay in his cattleshed. There, strangers among strangers, they found God was with them.

Loneliness is not so much a matter of *isolation* from people as it is of *insulation* against God. Joseph and Mary had removed all insulation; they knew that God was there.

The little town of Bethlehem, infested by crowds of lonely strangers, reminds us that when we seem most alone, we are really least alone. God is more likely to be revealed in a solitary, mangerlike quietness than in bustling crowds and clamorous streets. When lonely, look for God. He is near. Remember Bethlehem?

When you are discouraged, discontented with the quality of your thoughts and deeds, upset by your blundering, dismayed at the waywardness of your children, distressed by the disorder

89

and the dark outlook of the world, remember Bethlehem. Recall how the whole world seemed dressed in mourning-black on that First Christmas night. Remember how disheartening that faraway night must have seemed to the Jewish people, with Herod's oppressive troops marching through the streets, with Augustus Caesar demanding more taxes, with God's people virtual slaves to the pagan Romans.

Then remember the difference it made to Joseph and Mary and to shepherds and Wise Men to know that Christ was born. Recall how faith broke through their fear, frustration and despair when they realized with sudden force that God shares our humble setting with us, and we are not alone in our trials and testings. God is here.

The most powerful force in the world is not the threatening darkness, but what God is doing, quietly, almost secretly, in some unexpected way and in some surprising place, like in an out-of-the-way manger. Any simpleton would have believed that darkness had the final word in the world that first Christmas night. But the Wise Men believed in the Baby. So did Joseph and Mary and the shepherds. When discouraged, be wise. Remember Bethlehem's dark streets and the bright-eyed Baby who was God's Holy Reminder that nothing is hopeless when God is near.

Three little fellows were discussing their fathers. One declared, "My dad is an attorney. He practices law." Another said, "My father is a doctor. He practices medicine." The third child said, rather pensively, "My dad is a Christian. But he is not practicing it right now."

A practicing Christian is one who remembers Bethlehem in December and *always*. For Bethlehem reminds us of what we most need to know, that God cares enough for us to be near us.

26

$\mathscr{Help\ Us\ to\ See}$

(A Christmas Prayer)

O God,
Who once made a star to shine
In the darkness of a dismal world,
So that Wise Men might know
The Savior had come,
Give to us now
Wisdom and alertness of mind
To see stars of hope
Still shining.

Help us
To see that
The most hopeful Event in human history,
Christ's birth,
Came amidst hopelessness,
          and
The greatest Miracle of all
Was wrought amidst the commonplace
Of a lowly manger,
And that, even yet,
No darkness can dim His light
          and
No heart is too humble
To shelter Him.

Help us
To see that the blessed life that began
In a Babe in Bethlehem
Is still alive,
Still here,
Still real,
Still needing a home.

Help us
To see that
The Word made flesh in Christ
Can still express itself
In flesh today,
Our flesh,
Our lips,
Our hands.

Help us
To see that
One day, brimming full of joy,
Kindness, generosity and self-forgetting,
Can overflow into all our other days.

Help us
To see that
For those who seek Thy light
All darkness makes Thy stars shine brighter;
So give to us, now and always,
The upward look.

Open our eyes;
Open our minds;
Open our hearts
This Christmastime.
Keep them open
All our days.
Amen.

27

Open-Mindedness, Wise and Otherwise

In one respect open-mindedness is like faith, hope and love. They are virtues or vices, depending upon their goals and uses.

Some people have too much faith devoted to the wrong things. They have faith that if they flatter the right people, pull the proper strings and wield the right influences they can rise in the world without actually deserving a position of prominence.

Some have too much hope, living in breathless, expectant desire that the fellow on the next rung of the executive ladder above them will blunder, slip and fall so that they can seize his position.

Some love the wrong things, having too great a passion for popularity or money so that they will do anything and compromise any principle "to have and to hold" the object of their affections.

So with open-mindedness; its true value depends upon what a person is open to, what his mind is ready to receive and entertain. An old Mother Goose rhyme describes a cat's-eye view of London:

> *Pussy cat, pussy cat, where have you been?*
> *I've been to London to visit the Queen.*
> *Pussy cat, pussy cat, what did you there?*
> *I frightened a little mouse under a chair.*

WISE MEN

THE WISE MEN OF THE NATIVITY STORY ARE REFERRED TO IN THE GREEK, IN ST. MATTHE GOSPEL AS "μάγοι από άνατολων" OR "W MEN FROM THE EAST" (KING JAMES VERSION OUR WORD "MAGI" COMES FROM THE GREEK F SAGE, "μάγοι" BEING TRANSLATED "WISE ME

SCHOLARS DIFFER AS TO WHAT MANNER OF MEN THEY WERE, SOME BELIEVING THEM TO HAVE BEEN MEMBERS OF A PRIESTLY CASTE — SUCH AS SHAMANS ARE — AND SPECIALIZING IN THE INTERPRETATION OF DREAMS ○ OTHERS ARE CONVINCED THEY WERE PERSIAN PRIESTS OF THE ZORASTRIAN FAITH ○○○○☆○○ EARLY IN THE CHRISTIAN ERA THERE WERE JEWS WHO WERE CALLED "MAGI" AND WERE LIKELY SCHOLARS ATTACHED TO THE ROMAN COURTS ☆ ☆ SOME MAGI FROM EGYPT, BABYLONIA AND PER: WERE THOUGHT OF AS MAGICIANS ○

ST. MATTHEW'S GOSPEL MAKES NO EFFORT TO IDENTIFY THE WISE MEN — OR MAGI — EXCEF TO IMPLY THEY CAME FROM A GREAT DISTANCE SOMEWHERE EAST OF BETHLEHEM, AND TO INDI CATE THEY HAD STUDIED THE HEAVENS, AND H/ PLUMBED THE WONDROUS SECRET OF CHRIST' COMING WHICH WAS WRITTEN IN THE STARS

TRADITION TELLS US THE WISE MEN WERE KINGS ○ THIS LOVELY LEGEND WAS FOUNDED, PERHAPS, ON PSALMS 68:29 AND 72:10 WHICH TELL OF KINGS BEARING GIFTS ——— SUPPORTING THE IMPRESSION OF ROYAL WEALTH EXPRESSED IN ST. MATTHEW 2:11 : "○○○AND WHEN THEY HAD OPENED THEIR TREASURES, THEY PRESENTED UNTO HIM GIFTS: GOLD, AND FRANK- INCENSE, AND MYRRH○"

94

The cat in London had a splendid opportunity of seeing museums, national monuments, churches and cathedrals, the royal palace and the Queen and her court. But the cat had mice on its mind. It was receptive to mice, because mice counted most with that cat. Preoccupation with mice means open-mindedness toward rodents and a closed mind toward the splendors of the world.

In December I feel especially sorry for cats, dogs, birds and all other creatures whose minds are open to mice, bones and bird seed, but are closed to a certain star, a stable, a manger, awe-struck shepherds, Wise Men, Mary and Joseph and the Baby whose first cry split history into Before and After.

More important to religion than any particular statement of creed is the inner spirit and attitude of our faith. Essential to the life of faith is spiritual openness and hospitality to the highest truth, the most awe-inspiring beauty and the greatest goodness that have come to man, seeking a home. It is the central conviction of the Christian faith that in the birth of Jesus Christ the Highest has revealed Himself.

Does "putting Christ into Christmas" mean keeping commercial considerations out of it? Hardly! Shopping and gift exchange, if they are but minor notes of Christmas, lend to the happy melody of the month. But Christmastime can and should be far more than a time of extraordinary commercial traffic and high expenditures. We easily become so immersed in planning, purchasing, wrapping and exchanging gifts that we give little thought to the Savior's birth and to the difference that Baby has made in the world, and to what He means to us personally.

Being too open-minded to the material celebration of Christmas means being close-minded to its spiritual significance. If it is tragic to go to London and see only mice, while missing the splendors of the palace and the Queen's court, it is still more pitiable to go through December, seeing loaded store counters, choice gifts and wrappings, bright lights on tinseled trees, and fail to find the Little One who has made such a big difference that we have divided all history at the moment of His birth.

Soon packages will be arriving at your door marked "DO NOT OPEN UNTIL CHRISTMAS." My greatest wish for the world this season is that all minds everywhere would be *open until Christmas,* and always, to the spirit and the message of the One whose coming we joyfully celebrate.

28

Let Thy Light Shine Tonight

God of the Holy Land far away,
  Of Bethlehem over the sea,
Whose star sparkled over a manger,
  Let Thy light shine tonight on me.

God of the cattle stall long ago,
  Lord of the Babe asleep,
God of the wise men travelling slow,
  Lord of the shepherds and sheep,
God of good Joseph and Mary
  And the unnamed people who came,
The rich and poor, to the stable door
  To honor the Savior's birth,
Like the radiance that poured
  From the Christmas star
Let Thy love fall tonight on earth.

God of the holy lands very near,
  The lands of pine and birch,
God of the humblest cabin home
  And the little village church,
God of the Northland and the East,
  Lord of the deer and manger beast,
God of the snowclad evergreen,
  Lord of the palms we have never seen,
God of the distant and the near,
  Of every age and every place,
Lord of Christmas and common days,
  Send Thy gentle, starlike grace
Wherever human hearts abide
  That make room for the Christ inside.

29

May Christmas Time Be His Time

(A Christmas Prayer)

Our Heavenly Father, we thank Thee that, although many centuries have come and gone since Christ was born among us, the story of His coming has never been lost. It is always new, untarnished by the telling, undimmed by the passing years.

We rejoice in the glad remembrances of that first Christmas: gentle Mary, her eyes and cheeks aglow with gladness; Joseph, calm, proud, standing guard among the friendly shadows of the cattle stall; awe-struck shepherds listening to angel songs coming from a rift in heaven where a star peeps through; Wise Men, faithfully following the light of the star to that quiet manger-place, apart from the thronging world; and amidst it all, center of it all, the meaning of it all, the Christ Child, born to be the Savior.

We thank Thee, our Father, for this holy season when our souls travel the road to Bethlehem. We confess our need to go there. It is peaceful in the cattle stall, and our clamorous spirits crave to rest awhile in such a sacred silence. It is worshipful there where Christ is found, where shepherds and Wise Men kneel in holy wonder. We need to worship, to regain the heavenly perspective, to rediscover what is truly best and highest in Thy world. While on our knees at the manger we find the Best Gift Thou hast sent us.

God of ancient Bethlehem, Lord of modern city streets, hear our confession. Our hearts have often been busy inns, too full of thronging guests, so that when Thy Holy One has come, seeking room, He has found no resting place in us. Forgive our excessive busyness. Forgive our preoccupation with little things. Keep us ever mindful that Thy truth, grace and goodness are *always* looking for a home. Grant us the insight to recognize Thy holy ones when we see them, to know they are Thine, to welcome them joyfully and to make our hearts their dwelling places.

98

Forgive, O God, our self-imposed poverty of spirit. Like shepherds on Judean hills, we have our work to do, our possessions to watch over and care for, but unlike those shepherds, we live amidst Thy wonders without sensing them.

Forgive us for our meager awareness of Thy dealings with us, for the dullness of soul that permits us to go about earth's business while angel voices softly sing "Joy to the world! The Lord has come!" and we do not hear the song, or the rustle of angel wings, or thrill to the excitement that fills the air.

Let us not miss the Christmas clues Thou hast given concerning Thy divine intentions. Let us see that Thy light is meant to shine upon this humble earth and touch every common thing with holiness. May we remember that there is nothing so small and nothing so poor but that it becomes sacred when brought as a gift to Christ. Let us dare to believe that He who forgives a cattle stall's dirt floor and pardons the pitiful plainness of a manger bed, may bless our shabby hearts with His presence and fill our sorry days to overflowing with His love, joy and peace.

O Thou who didst bless Bethlehem on that far-off starlit night, bless all the cities of earth and all the homes of the world at this Christmastime. Remember in mercy the hungry people of all nations — those hungry for food, for friendship, for a few pain-free moments, for love, for joy, for peace, for God. Let the hungry be filled.

Bless all whose lives are too full of Christmas celebrations to be mindful of Christ. Let not the Babe of Bethlehem be lost amidst commemorations of His birth, hidden beneath holly wreaths and evergreen trees, or suffocated under mounds of gifts and heaps of Christmas wrappings. May Christmas time be His time, Christmas Day His day, when Christ gets a new chance to live in us.

Father, Thou hast made one season especially glad and one night incomparably bright with the memory of Christ's birth. Now, once more, small candles of hope flicker on the windowsills of our hearts to bid Christ welcome here.

Let Him come again.

Let Him stay.

Amen.

30

Shall We Give Him a Home?

Among the world's most pitiable people are those who cannot receive. Life's splendid favors are offered to them, but they cannot accept these gifts.

The deaf, for example, live in the midst of sounds as do people with perfect hearing. At this blessed season beloved Christmas carols fill the air; bells ring; "Merry Christmas" is shouted from doorways and street corners; children laugh in wild, gleeful abandon as they anticipate glad Christmas surprises; the Nativity Story is read around family circles and from countless pulpits; the loveliest truth the world has known is told concerning God's self-disclosure in Infant flesh. The sweetest sounds of earth are falling upon their ears, but the deaf do not hear. They are unable to receive these gifts.

The blind, as well as those who see, live amidst this season's visual beauties, but they cannot receive such favors of loveliness and wonder.

The Gospel of Luke tells why Christ was born in a cattle stall, saying of Mary, "And she brought forth her firstborn son, and wrapped him in swaddling clothes, and laid him in a manger; because there was no room for them in the inn." We know little about the Bethlehem innkeeper, and what we do know is sad. On that holy night his rooms were all taken. There was no more space. Royalty was coming. The Infant King would be born at any hour. But the innkeeper could not receive Him.

The innkeeper's fault is a familiar one, for the inability to receive is one of life's most common tragedies. Too often the Best must be turned away from our inn because our capacity is limited, and we are already full. We are limited in time, and all of us restricted to the same degree. All of us, the busy and the idle alike, have the same number of hours in the day. No one has more than twenty-four; no one has less. It is as if we were all innkeepers with the same size inns and the same number of rooms. When these rooms are full, additional guests are turned away. We can receive no more.

Our reading time is limited. We cannot read everything. If we fill reading hours with trash there will be no room for books that stretch the mind and elevate the spirit.

Time for conversation is confined on all sides by duties that demand attention. If we gossip or find fault or trifle, there will be no room for discussion of meaningful matters, for saying the word of encouragement, hope or cheer, or the word of gratitude and appreciation.

Surely one of the chief problems of modern man hearkens back to the first Christmas and beyond it, to man's pre-occupation with less important things, so that when the Highest comes to man's door it must be turned away. The place is already full.

One other observation should be made concerning the inn at Bethlehem: its fullness was no worse than complete emptiness would have been. Had the inn been empty, Joseph and Mary would not have lodged there anyway. When a city is overflowing with crowds, as was Bethlehem that night, and an inn has no guests, it is because the place is locked up on account of bankruptcy or pestilence, or it has failed because of its bad reputation. The too full and the too empty inns are equally inhospitable to guests.

But there is a wholesome kind of fullness, a spiritual kind, that is far different from Bethlehem's inn on that long ago Holy Night. It is a cordial, hospitable fullness. It somehow manages to provide enough room when the Highest appears and asks for lodging. There is a marked difference between the physical world and the spiritual at this

point. In the material and temporal realm the empty container is the one that stands ready to receive: the empty glass is ready for the milk; the empty cup is prepared for coffee; the empty room has space for a guest. But where souls are concerned emptiness is undesirable. Our Christmas guests would be disappointed to come to empty homes. A royal welcome is given when the house is occupied with excited, expectant people, glad that the honored guest has at last arrived. The house that is full of friendly feeling, brimming with cheer, conversation and laughter, provides a glad welcome.

Similarly, it is the occupied mind that makes room for new knowledge. An empty mind gives new information no more than a grudgeful recognition, while a mind full of good things gladly greets further enlightenment and additional truth and gives them a home.

Or, consider the person without close friends; as far as companionship is concerned his inn is empty. He may rationalize his friendlessness, protesting that he likes to be independent; he doesn't need friends; people make him nervous. "If you don't trust people, they can't hurt you," he may say. One might think that such a person would have plenty of room for friends, since his life is so empty. But the opposite is so. The person whose life is already full of friends is the kind who can always make room for more.

Innkeepers whose inns are empty react to Christ's coming as badly as do those whose lives are too crowded. Both turn the Holy One away.

How, then, should we manage our inns? We should keep our hearts open to all the beauty, truth and goodness that come our way, for they — like Joseph and Mary — are looking for room. They need a place to stay. Then when that most beautiful Life, highest Truth and greatest Goodness tries to get a new start in the world, in us, let us give Him a chance.

31

A Bit of Heaven in Your Thinking

Now the old year fades. It drifts away and vanishes like a wisp of breath upon the frosty air. And man is the only mortal being that notices the old year's passing. Among all of God's creatures man is the only one that cares to count the years, the days and the moments as they pass. The chickadee at our bird feeder, the fox that trots along our woodland trail, the deer that browses beneath our birches are immersed in the same time sequence that engulfs us all, but they know nothing about marking off the years or recording the days and hours. When the old year ends, nothing in wild nature will mark its close. No salvo of thunder will signal a change. No celestial fireworks will salute the old year's going or the new year's coming. But man will ring bells, blow whistles and shout greetings at midnight on December thirty-first, for he is earth's time-conscious creature, the only earthly being aware of a fleeting mortality, the only one to watch calendars and to manufacture clocks. Man is God's time-enamoured and time-panicked creature.

We love time. We plead for more time as if it were life's most precious commodity. When people attempt to hurry us we beg, "For heaven's sake, give me time!" We speak optimistically, affectionately, and often mistakenly, about time: "Time heals all things"; time is "the father of truth."

Yet, in spite of our love for time, we fear it, too. The unchanging pace and relentless rush of time's passing push us toward nervous ruin. A New York specialist in mental disorders has declared that civilized man's three greatest killers are not heart disease, cancer and accidents. Rather, he contends, they are the calendar, which reminds us of deadline dates; the telephone, which fatigues and frays the nerves with its demanding jangle; the clock, which constantly reminds us, "Hurry! Hurry!" So modern man fears the thing he loves, and is brought to the brink of nervous destruction by a faculty that makes him unique among his fellow inhabitants of the earth — his sense of time.

How can we best make use of time, so that it becomes the servant of our highest interests rather than a cruel master, driving us toward madness?

Learn to handle the year a day at a time, thus making big opportunities and great problems more manageable. Regret for yesterday's failures, added to anxiety about the tomorrows, plus concern for today's needs make too heavy a burden for anyone to carry. Perhaps God gave us our years a day at a time because such small parcels are proportionate to our strength.

All our days will be significant, rather than frenzied, if we remember that each moment we live we are becoming something more or something less than what we already are. "Boys will be boys," we sometimes say as we excuse a youngster's prankish misbehavior. But boys won't be boys for long. Soon they will be men. And young men become older men, and older men soon go the way of all flesh. We are all changing; we are all on our way elsewhere. What counts most is the direction of the change, for worse or for better. A sound use of time is to invest it in self-improvement, molding tomorrow's character by being all we should be and doing all we should do today, by God's grace.

Measure your life by a higher standard than the clock on your mantle or the watch on your wrist. The world's finest precision clocks are tested by Greenwich time, which is kept at Greenwich Observatory in England. Each night Greenwich clocks are checked against the stars and corrected by testing them against the movements of the earth in relation to heavenly bodies that are millions of light years away. Scientists get true time from the skies.

So do we. While we may not understand God any more than the astronomers fully comprehend the mysteries of distant stars, still we know enough about God to set our lives by. We believe God spends His eternities creating better worlds, making better people and making people better, and doing all that He does in love. Setting our lives by the heavens means to invest our time making the world a bit better where we live, being (and helping others to be) better people, and doing all in the spirit of love for God and man.

Many of us will start the new year with a glance at the clock. We will do better to look beyond clocks and get a bit of heaven into our thinking.

32

The Real Thing

Bishop Bruce Baxter once told of a small boy who had begged for a horse for Christmas. His father tried to dissuade him, saying that a horse was hardly the ideal pet for a city boy.

But the lad would not listen to reason. "I don't want anything else for Christmas but a horse," he insisted.

The father bought the youngster a beautifully painted picture of a horse. When the lad unwrapped the picture on Christmas morning he was crestfallen and cried, "Daddy, this isn't a real horse! It's just a picture." So, after Christmas the father returned the painting to the store and tried to please the boy by buying him an expensive, well-illustrated book about horses — wild horses, work horses, race horses, show horses. Again the lad was disappointed and claimed, "These aren't real horses. They're only horse stories and horse pictures."

Then the boy's father bought him a toy horse that stood taller than the youngster's head. Surely this would please him. But when he saw it, the boy summed up his disappointment and chagrin, saying, "I want a real horse that's made out of horse!"

That boy's insistence on the real thing deserves our understanding.

At the beginning of a new year, one of the most probing questions we can ask ourselves is this: "Do I know well enough what I want out of life, so that I will settle for no cheap substitute?" In this age of artificiality we would all do well to stubbornly insist on much more of the real thing.

There should be an insistence on love that is really love. Our society offers many substitutes, gracing poor counterfeits with the good name "love." Superficial people claim they have "fallen in love" with someone of the opposite sex whenever they feel a surge of emotion upon having a casual encounter with an attractive face and figure. That is as shallow and perverted as calling a curse a "prayer," simply because the blasphemy contains the word "God." Prayer may utter the word "God," but it is much more than that. Love between the sexes may contain much desire. But it is more.

Again, what some people call "love" may be but a neurotic need to dominate, or be dominated, the need to belong or to possess. Many a time "I love you" really means "I love *me,* and want you to make me happy."

Real love means having in common with another person a community of ideas, moral standards and tastes. It means finding more joy in company with that person than with anyone else. Real love is responsiveness to another person's needs. It is also pride in what another is and does. Real love means giving time, attention, tender care and a touch of happiness, without demanding reward.

One great need of our civilization, if the sanctity of the home is to be preserved, is to teach the young what real love is, and to persuade them to reject all substitutes.

Moreover, we can insist upon living a real life, rather than enduring mere existence. When some people say they live in New York, Oklahoma, Texas, Ontario, Europe or anywhere else, they are mistaken. They merely exist there. And existence is but a cheap substitute for real living. Living things, say the biologists, feed, change and grow, and tend to reproduce themselves. Living souls do, too. They find meat and drink in great thoughts and ideals. They hungrily seek the good, the true and the beautiful.

Living souls change for the better, growing in moral stature, becoming more understanding of others, more loving, more helpful as the years roll by. They compete with what they were yesterday, and improve on their previous records. Stagnation is not living. Life that is real living changes for the better with the changing years.

And vitally alive souls reproduce themselves. That is to say, others live because a person of real spiritual vitality has given them a start. Such a person is like a candle that is used to light other candles; like a small fire used to kindle other fires. To be like that is real living.

As we begin the new year, and as we commence each day, let's face reality. Let us ask ourselves, "What is my real purpose, my real goal, my real work? How can I demonstrate real love? How can I really live?"

No cheap substitutes!

Let's start being real people.

33

Crisis and Character

From where I sit writing I can see flames in the fireplace consuming logs of white birth, sugar maple and white ash that I piled there a short while ago. The sweet gums, resins and scented oils that have been imprisoned in the wood cells are freed by the fire and they now fill the room with a woodsy perfume.

There is an old belief about firewood, that when it is ablaze it gives back all the colors that went into the making of the tree from which the wood is taken. Look into the fire, say the old-timers, and you will see the pale greens and purples of a thousand dawns, bright gold flashes of sun-flooded noons and the crimson of countless sunsets. Look again and you will behold the silver sheen of moonlit nights and the sparkling of a million stars. Until the wood is ignited it refuses to reveal its secret beauty. Wood is never fully known until it burns.

Perhaps the old belief about wood ablaze can illumine and warm our thought about man and his troubles. This is what a searing crisis does to us; it enables us to give back to the world all the colors of character that have been hidden away in us during more peaceful hours. Testings and trials show the stuff of which we are made.

This is good news about life's emergencies, rather than a solemn warning; it is glad gospel, rather than dark admonition. Testings reveal the best as well as the worst. Too often we see life's crises as threatening, menacing ogres bent on crushing us, from which we must escape at all costs. But difficulties can be as glorious as they are inevitable. They light up human nature, show the secret courage, liberate the strength that easy, peaceful days have held in bondage and bring a live luster to loyalties that have become dull through lack of testing. Crises are "moments of truth" concerning character.

The heroic Robert E. Lee was never greater than in defeat,

when he gave up his sword and with a dignity and forgiveness of his enemies that are rare on this earth sought to heal "the nation's wounds" and to find some path of usefulness for the few years he had left. Offered fifty thousand dollars for the use of his good name in a business enterprise, he refused and instead accepted the presidency of a small, struggling college at a salary of fifteen hundred dollars a year, because the school needed him. Frustration and hardship revealed in Robert E. Lee traits of character that tranquil days had left hidden.

While Abraham Lincoln had shown traces of greatness in earlier life, the epic proportions of the man's character were unguessed until he experienced the tragedy and grief of the Rebellion. Then, suffering long in the fire of civil conflict, the man Lincoln was more clearly manifested. The war that Lincoln dreaded and hated disclosed his stubbornness of purpose, his identification of himself with the suffering on both sides of the conflict, his freedom from bitterness, his awesome magnanimity of thought, desire and act, his clean, strong insistence upon generosity to his enemies. The light and warmth of the Lincoln whose qualities were unsealed by war still bless the lives of men everywhere.

In many churches a frequently used prayer begins with the phrase, "O God, unto whom all hearts are open, all desires known and from whom no secrets are hid . . ." All too often this prayer is interpreted to mean only that God knows the humiliating, shameful secrets of our hearts. Of course God knows them. But this is because God knows all about us, including the bad and the good. Together with all mankind we stand before His constant judgment. But it is a just judgment, mixed with generous mercy and liberal love. God sees us as we are, but that includes the hidden good as well as secret sins. Even the Day of Judgment of which the Bible speaks was intended not simply to strike terror into sinners but to signify that a glad day is coming when concealed worth and secret goodness will be uncovered.

The secrets that are not hidden from God, the hidden things God will yet reveal about His children, include the most beautiful values in all creation. Among these glorious secrets are the sacrifices parents have made for children without ever mentioning them. Some people have quietly suffered heavy losses of money, sleep, health and life for others, without publicity, credit

110

or complaint. But God knows. Others have sent to the needy anonymous gifts and have saved life and pride and brightened hope. God knows.

Then, too, there are the hasty, unkind words that have burst upon the brain of husband and wife, of parent or child in time of family conflict, but never reached the lips because they were stopped by the intervention of a compelling tenderness. God knows.

There are those whose handicaps have slowed them down and forced them off the fast expressway of modern existence, and they have made lovely the lonely, ugly detours they were compelled to take. God knows those detours.

And God knows the silent, secret prayers sent heavenward for our sakes by friends and acquaintances we never knew were God-inclined and who we never knew cared so much for us. Yes, God knows and someday in His own good time will unveil the covered goodness.

Difficulties are our minor Judgment Days when the real qualities of mind and soul are expressed. We can thank God for occasional emergencies that reveal what we are, both bad and good, and what needs amendment.

Maybe the Lord lets us get burnt once in a while because it is the only time we show our true colors.

LINCOLN   LEE

34

Living Above Discouragement

We need hardship.

Occasional trouble, and even defeat, are not necessarily enemies of the good life. Rather they often stimulate development of hidden potentials that we would not otherwise discover. This is true in the realm of nature. While many people who can afford to do so flee the hardships of winter in North America, scientists have demonstrated that "a cold spell" is absolutely necessary for some forms of life. Eggs of a few species of insects will not hatch unless first frozen. Some seeds require many weeks of sub-freezing cold if they are to sprout in the springtime. Some plants will blossom only after extended periods of exposure to the cold. Certain species of apple trees refuse to bud properly unless they have been exposed to nine hundred or more hours of temperatures below forty-five degrees Fahrenheit.

While personality is basically formed early in life, character comes to its finest flowering only after enduring trouble. Read the lives of the heroic leaders of any nation — the Churchills, Gandhis, Nehrus, the Washingtons, Lincolns and Lees — and you will discover that, before they emerged into positions of great prominence, the best of them suffered periods of painful struggle against grim odds.

Much of the time General George Washington was leading the Continental Army during the Revolutionary War, the Continental Congress was unwilling or unable to raise enough troops and sufficient money to support Washington's armed forces.

Writing from Valley Forge in January, 1778, Washington reported that only 572 of the 17,000 men in camp were fit for duty. "Unless there is a great and capital change, this army must be inevitably reduced to one or the other of these three things; starve, dissolve, or disperse in order to obtain subsistence in the best manner they possibly can." Many of the men were seriously ill. Thousands were nearly naked, or wrapped up in sacking.

In addition to the slowness of Congress to act on behalf of the army, Washington knew of wide discontent with his leadership. John Adams, who would one day succeed Washington as President, expressed the envy and opposition of many when on the floor of Congress he rebuked "the superstitious veneration that is sometimes paid to General Washington." A clique of Washington's subordinate officers, together with certain members of Congress, wanted to humiliate him by replacing him as Commander-in-chief with Horatio Gates. Moreover, Washington's small, ill-equipped forces often met mortifying defeat at the hands of the British.

Still George Washington endured and triumphed and illustrated one of life's fundamental truths: greatness is in large part the ability to rise above the discouragements by which the world tries to swamp our spirits.

What central convictions make the good and great of the world persist in their purposes in spite of crushing hardships? The undiscourageable know that:

Defeat sometimes serves better than victory to teach us life's valuable lessons, and failure often jolts the soul and spills the splendor out;

The capacity to fail is a part of greatness: worms and snakes cannot stumble and fall, but man can;

Failure in a cause that will finally triumph is better than success in a cause that will finally fail;

Public ridicule and applause are, alike, but passing phases in the life of any servant of the common good, and one should no more let ridicule depress one's spirits than let applause be too gratifying. Neither is a measure of ultimate defeat or success;

When we cannot move forward as far as we would like, we ought to take every step we can, even if it is only one, for action often lifts foul moods of despair;

No man is God; therefore no man should assume God's prerogatives and responsibilities of trying to run the entire universe;

God has placed more power within us and around us than we ever use, and one secret of living the life of trust is to "plug into the universe," as someone has put it — which really

113

means to live in constant, conscious communion with the God of power and love.

Strengthened by such convictions concerning God and man, the great of the world have used hardship as preparation for victories over themselves and opposing forces in the world. And such convictions are available to every one of us.

35

Our Will and God's

The devout sometimes make fools of themselves by pretending to know too much about the will of God. Too easily man projects his own reluctances, prejudices, anxieties and fears onto Heaven, saying of something he dislikes, "It is not God's will."

Most religious people of the western world now accept vaccination against diseases as a great blessing. But when vaccination was first proposed as a means of preventing epidemics of disease, there was a noisy hue and cry that men were attempting to defeat the will of God. If God wanted His children to be sick, medicine should not get in God's way.

Vaccination was new in George Washington's day. As a young man, Washington himself had been afflicted by smallpox, and his handsome face was severely pitted with scars of the disease. When he was near the height of his power and glory, Washington learned of the benefits of vaccination and became an enthusiastic supporter of inoculation. But for all his evangelistic zeal, he could muster few followers. Although he had led armies to victory in the Revolutionary battles of Trenton and Princeton, and the colonies were grateful to him, all of his prestige and authority were required to get the practice of inoculation against smallpox adopted in the army. Even after his soldiers were vaccinated, his critics declared that Washington's later defeats in the fighting season of 1777 were due to the General's terrible sin in interfering with the clear will of

114

God. Critics claimed God had willed that men become afflicted with smallpox, and by having soldiers inoculated, Washington was defeating God's intentions. Therefore, God sent military disaster as punishment.

Dr. Lyman Beecher, the famed clergyman and father of Henry Ward Beecher and Harriet Beecher Stowe, was once embarrassed by his assumptions that he was privy to the will of God. A neighborhood church that he regarded as unorthodox caught fire and burned to the ground. Dr. Beecher boldly declared in his sermon on the next Sunday that the calamity was God's judgment on false doctrine. Before the week was up, Lyman Beecher's church also burned and was nearly a total loss. (Wouldn't you like to have heard Beecher's *next* sermon?)

The Biblical faith is not based upon man's confidence that he clearly knows *all* about the will of God, but rather that all men can know *enough* of God's will to live better than we live by human wisdom alone, and enough to win God's approval.

How, then, shall we seek to fathom the will of God?

First, pray. We can no more know the mind of God by merely thinking about or talking about God than we can know the mind of a person by thinking or talking about him. To know a person well we must think *with* him and talk *with* him, in intimate companionship. Prayer is fellowship, conversation with God, and attentiveness when God speaks.

Second, discuss the matter with the wisest, noblest, most devout person you know, for God sometimes sends us messages through His closest friends. But do not regard even the wisest person as the infallible spokesman of God.

Third, while you are waiting for God's answer, go on performing your common tasks and fulfilling your everyday duties to the best of your ability. Sometimes it is in the midst of the most unattractive, commonplace duties that God speaks to us most clearly, as He spoke to Moses while Moses tended sheep in a wilderness, calling him to lead Israel out of bondage.

Fourth, if the moment arrives when you simply must act before you are certain of God's will, then act according to the best light you presently have. Do so in the confidence that God honors our best choices and our best work, even when it is imperfect.

115

Fifth, dare to believe that it is best when sometimes the Divine Will overrules our will, as when a kindly parent refuses to let his little child play with matches or razor blades. God has dealings with us that are often beyond our understanding and liking, but they are always for our good.

Sixth, once you have acted according to the best lights you have, waste no thought or emotion on self-recrimination and regret. If your best seems unsuccessful, remember that some great defeats God gloriously uses in a way that shames and shadows earth's victories.

Remember that cross on a hill?

Springtime Holidays

-HK-

36

Stormy Weather

Why is the weather so tempestuous in the springtime? It is because the season cannot make up its mind.

Springtime is not clearly one thing or another, either winter or summer. The season seems unable to decide which it will be, so it vacillates back and forth. Some days it chooses warmth. The sun comes out from behind leaden clouds. Coldness yields. Snow melts. Brooks sing. Summery south winds make the days tender. Then spring impulsively indulges its taste for winter. The air is chilled. Snowflakes fall from bleak skies. The marsh that has awakened to the spring peeper's song falls silent, hurt by winter's careless blow. Earth and skies will become more settled when the weather renounces its fickleness, makes a choice between winter and summer, and is loyal to its decision.

Indecision is the soul's stormy weather. It is miserable. Some people plan their lives so as to find what peace of mind they can by reducing hesitation to a minimum. Florenz Ziegfield, the noted theatrical producer, liked candy and kept a large box of licorice drops on his desk. When a friend observed, "I didn't know you liked licorice drops," Ziegfield replied, "I don't particularly. But they're all black, and I don't have to make up my mind which color is best."

We cannot play Ziegfield's little game with life in general. Life's colors are not all black, and its flavors are not all licorice. Life's choices are multi-colored and of many tastes. Whether we like it or not, whether we are profoundly frustrated or not, some selections must be made among all the possibilities confronting us.

The New Testament vividly pictures Pontius Pilate as a stormy soul who could not make a choice. The Gospels tell us that just before His crucifixion Jesus was taken by His enemies before Pilate, procurator of Judea, who held office under Tiberius

Caesar. Tiberius was a tough emperor who would excuse no rebellions or civil unrest in the Roman provinces, and Jesus was accused by His enemies of treason against the Roman Empire. If the accusation was valid Pilate was obligated to punish the prisoner. But when Pilate examined Jesus he found no evidence that the charge was true. So Pilate sought to free the accused. Jesus' enemies insisted that He was guilty and must die.

Pilate then attempted to find some way of making no decision at all. He sent Jesus to Herod, hoping Herod would decide what should be done with Him. But Herod returned Christ to Pilate. Then Pilate gave the crowd a choice between Barabbas, a zealot and a murderer, and Christ; he would free one or the other. The crowd chose to free Barabbas and kill Christ. At last, Pilate ordered Christ scourged, and He was lacerated by whips to which were tied sharp fragments of bone. Then Pilate presented Christ to the crowd, thinking that such a humbling and painful punishment might satisfy the people. But His enemies were still insistent that Christ be slain.

At last Pilate could stall no longer. He was in authority. Christ was Pilate's "affair" as well as a victim of the crowd. Mark's gospel says, "Pilate, wishing to satisfy the crowd, released for them Barabbas; and having scourged Jesus, he delivered him to be crucified." So he let others make the big decision after all! He washed his hands of the whole matter and cravenly blamed the ugly business on the Jews. Yet, in spite of hesitancy, maneuvering and hand-washing, Pilate played his part in Christ's crucifixion.

Here is the real drama of every life: fate rests in the choices we refuse to make as well as in those we deliberately make. By refusing to make a responsible choice Pilate let Christ die fully as much as if he had decided the Nazarene was guilty and had hatefully condemned Him to the cross.

Hesitate while crossing a busy thoroughfare and you are hurt or killed just as certainly as if you determined to be careless or to die. Hesitate too long about stopping at the railroad crossing to let a train go by and you are courting death as much as if you had chosen to "race" the train to the crossing. To make no choice of good reading for the sake of the mind's enrichment is the same as refusing to read the best; either way the best does not get read.

To refuse to choose Christ, as Pilate did, is the same as rejecting Him. Either way Christ suffers the same fate.

Pilate dodged his responsibilities, but he could not dodge the *consequences* of dodging his responsibilities. Neither can we.

37

What Is So Special About the Death of Jesus?

Since the beginnings of recorded history, countless men and women have been executed by hanging, strangling, drowning, burning, shooting and on crosses. Many innocent men endured the agonies of crucifixion under Roman rule. But we give little thought and spend no time commemorating their awful deaths.

Yet one death has caught and held the world's attention from the moment the Victim drew His final breath. And two thousand years after the event millions sing of the instrument of Christ's execution:

> *In the cross of Christ I glory,*
> *Towering o'er the wrecks of time;*
> *All the light of sacred story*
> *Gathers round its head sublime.*

No such hymn was ever composed about a hangman's rope or a lethal gas chamber. At first the cross was not a holy thing to Christ's disciples. On that first Good Friday the cross was as gruesome as a hangman's noose or an electric chair would be to us, and Christ's death seemed to be the extinction of their highest hopes as well as the end of their Dearest Friend.

But Easter changed all that, and the cross became the symbol of a courageous, crusading faith, and Christ's death became the world's clearest revelation of God's love and care.

What is so special about the death of Christ that it is not only mourned by millions each year on Good Friday, but it is even celebrated in song — as if the world could not free itself of that cross once planted on Calvary? We are repelled by the ugliness of it and attracted by the meaning of it. And attraction is the more powerful emotion. Once it pulled a small crowd to Calvary. Some came because they were ordered to nail Him there. Others came out of curiosity and morbidity, some to ridicule and jeer, and a few were drawn by love and loyalty.

The powerful magnetism of the cross still grows. Explain it as you will, the gallows of the Galilean now draws millions of us to Calvary and holds us there as if we had an awful personal interest and involvement in the One dying there, as if it were our sins He was bearing, our penalty He was paying, our pain He was feeling, our death He was dying, as if our Loved One died there for His loved ones.

That tremendous, mysterious dimension is lacking in the death of other men. While others have died for us in war, in fighting fire, in medical experimentation and exploration, as martyrs in the cause of religion and patriotism, of no one else in all the world have so many said so meaningfully, "He died for me."

Isn't this, then, the primary reason we see Christ's death as "special," because we are all in some way involved in it? We never ask, "Were you there when they beheaded Charles I of England?" or "Were you there when the guillotine descended on the neck of Marie Antoinette of France?" In their deaths we do not feel personally involved. But millions sing the Negro spiritual:

Were you there when they crucified my Lord?
Were you there when they crucified my Lord?
Oh, sometimes it causes me to tremble, tremble.
Were you there when they crucified my Lord?

And the heart's answer is, "Yes, I was there. We were all there!" Each of us is involved in Christ's death in a way we are not implicated in the death of any other historical figure. Sins like our own put Christ there; for our sins He died. So we are deeply involved in Calvary.

Moreover, we are involved in the crucifixion because it is God's love for us that is revealed there. The real great, good news the cross brings to us is not of man's sinfulness but of God's goodness. In Christ's painful sacrifice for us we see God's suffering over us. The core of our faith is that God is Christlike, so we point to the Savior on His cross and say, "See! that is what God is like." The cross is history's terse summary of all the vast truths and the baffling, unfathomable mysteries concerning God's incalculable love for man; "For God so loved the world that he gave his only begotten Son that whosoever believeth on him should not perish, but have everlasting life."

Because each person in every generation desperately needs to be reminded of both his sin and his salvation, found in God's love, the cross remains a recurrent theme in the world. When Emile Zola, the French novelist, was unjustly condemned by his judges and his case was regarded as "closed," Zola's lawyer pointed to a crucifix and exclaimed, "Remember, gentlemen, that was once a closed case, too, but it was opened again." Christ's death has never remained a closed case. For our peace of mind, we sometimes wish it were marked "closed." But we cannot shake it from our minds, can we? Or from our hearts!

The cross remains. Whenever the strong victimize the weak, when the clever take unfair advantage of the ignorant, when the poor cry for bread, for medicine or shelter and are not heard, when men war against each other or persecute each other because of differences in color, nationality or creed, whenever we needlessly hurt ourselves or our fellowmen we give God pain, and the case of the cross is agonizingly reopened.

And whenever we wonder if God has forgotten us, there is that memorandum of God's brooding love and unceasing concern, stuck into a lonely hill and pointing Godward, signifying "You are remembered. See how much I care!"

Our case, as well as Christ's, is still open.

38

God's Plus Sign

A young painter loved to do full-length portraits of people, and she did them extremely well. When she was invited to display a collection of her paintings in a local store, many of her friends came to the exhibit. One day a professional painter stopped in, carefully examined the paintings, and then sought out the artist. After congratulating her on her skill he said, "I notice something most unusual about your work. Whenever you portray people, you paint them standing in long grass or in a pool of water."

"Yes, sir," agreed the girl.

"But why do you do that?"

"Well, it's like this," the girl replied. "I have never learned how to paint feet."

One reason more is not said about the cross of Christ from pulpits and in religious literature is that we have never mastered the mystery of it. We cannot capture the essence of it in words, nor can we comprehend its full meaning. John Milton wrote a beautiful ode, "On the Morning of Christ's Nativity," to celebrate the birth of Christ. Later he attempted to write a companion piece on the crucifixion of Christ but he gave it up. In Milton's published works one finds the beginning of the poem and a note that apologizes for its incompleteness, saying he could not find a satisfying way of expressing the meaning of Christ's death. The cross is a baffling riddle.

Yet, two thousand years after the crucifixion, Christ's cross stands in our memory, "towering o'er the wrecks of time." We can hardly ignore it. We must have some impressions of it. What are they?

Perhaps a child can help us find some meaning we might have missed in the cross. A little girl had arrived at a point in her schooling where she was admitted to the mysteries of mathematics. She was shown division signs, multiplication signs, minus signs and plus signs, and these symbols deeply impressed her. On the Sunday after she had learned about plus signs, the child accompanied her father to church. There she saw the golden cross on the altar, as she had seen it many times before. But this time, the appearance of the cross startled her and she whispered to her father, "Daddy! What is that plus sign doing on the altar?"

The girl's question was a natural one and more perceptive than she knew. In a profound sense the cross *is* God's plus sign. What is it doing in our churches and in our lives?

The cross means we are not alone in our toil, troubles and tragedies. God's love is with us in our disappointments, defeat, and death. In the midst of temptations toward bitter despair we can say, "Here am I, plus God's love and care." The cross of the Christ means that.

The cross signifies we are not alone in our sinning. Many of our actions, whether deliberate or unwitting, grow out of weaknesses, hatred and prejudices that are opposed to God's love and will for all of his children. The cross is God's way of saying to man, "I hate what you are doing, but you are my child. I love you, and I am with you." You can't even sin without God, for He is near, observing, caring, suffering, as when any good parent sees a child go wrong. The God who could be no better than to be like Christ speaks through the Figure on the cross, saying, "See what I am like! I care this much, to suffer when I need not, to show you I am with you even in your sinning." Not only when we are at our best is God with us, but when we are at our *worst* He is there — suffering to redeem us. Man plus sin plus God's mercy in Christ equals redemption.

Yet, the addition of the cross to life is not "simple addition," like adding one apple to one apple and getting two apples, or adding one apple and one orange and getting two pieces of fruit. It is more like adding hydrogen to oxygen and getting another substance altogether — water. As St. Paul put it "... If any man be in Christ, he is a new creature: old things are passed away; behold all old things are become new." Both components are changed. He who is "in Christ" has a new Center, new meaning, new desires, values, purposes and behavior; and Christ Himself gets a new, unique expression in the world through a life that has never been here before and will never be here again.

The forgiveness of God is the most healing revelation in the history of the world. Millions of people are suffering from sup-

125

pressed, subconscious, unrecognized feelings of guilt. They cannot be helped by the admonition, "It's all right this time. Just don't do it again." It is never enough to bring the suppressed feelings to the surface of the mind to analyze them, to salve and soothe them by advising, "Other people have done it too, and worse things than you have done others have done." The Church does more than bring unrecognized feelings to consciousness. Rather, the Church points to the cross of Christ and to the One hanging there, begging in agony, "Father, forgive them for they know not what they do," and the Church announces, "You see, you have not been able to forgive yourself, but He forgives you."

The cross, then, means hope. It says, "You need not stay the way you are." You, just as you are, plus God's redeeming power equal the person you were meant to be. The crucifixion is history's incomparable blood transfusion that pours Christ's life and perfect goodness into man's poor sin-fected condition, turning our waxen pallor into the glow of life, quickening the soul's failing pulse and awakening the comatose consciousness that had become unaware of God's mercy. We are never so spiritually alive and healthy as when we are connected to that Man on the cross.

How else does the Christ on the cross affect us? He is the "plus" in our lives that gives us a new beginning. A great gain was made recently in the conservation of our forests when a process was discovered whereby old newspapers could be reclaimed. For many years con-

126

servationists had been worried about the rate manufacturers of newsprint were using woodpulp for newspapers. Forests could be spared to some extent if only there were some way of reusing old newspapers. But how could the old printer's ink be removed? Then chemists devised a way of grinding up old newsprint and reducing it to pulp, adding a chemical that dissolved the printer's ink and starting all over again with clean paper.

Life imprints upon us all some things that should not be there, some of it false, some profane, some trivial, some bitter or sour. We need to be cleaned up so that we can begin all over again. Christ's life outpoured into ours does this for us. The old life fades out, and we have a new and different story to tell to the world.

When Socrates the Wise heroically died in ancient Athens, his friends were sure the world was made poorer by that philosopher's death. But, since Jesus died on a wretched cross just outside Jerusalem, His friends have been certain the world has been infinitely richer for His sacrifice.

It doesn't make sense, does it? But it makes a great Gospel!

39

Easter Reminds Us

Forces of darkness
Must yield to the Light
As surely as
Black-Saturday night
Must
    yield
        to
            Easter
                Morning.

   ❀   ❀   ❀

Easter
    proclaims the good news
        that
Life's seeming defeats
Are more victorious
        than
Its apparent triumphs,
        that
Christ on His cross
    has more power
        than
Christ riding to the beat
    of the crowd's applause
        on
            Palm Sunday.

   ❀   ❀   ❀

Easter
    reminds us
        that
God's Truth can be abused,
Whipped with scourges,

Driven through the streets,
Nailed to a cross,
Thrust through with spears,
Pronounced dead,
Shrouded in grave clothes
     and
Consigned to a tomb.
But
God's Truth
  will rise again,
    alive and
      stronger
       than
        before.

      ❈   ❈   ❈

Easter
  celebrates the glad certainty
    that
God has unforgettably
  shown mankind
    that
The world at its worst
Can take God's Best
And make it suffer,
But can never destroy it.
When men sinfully crucify Christ
They defeat sin, not Christ;
When they put Him to death,
It is the death of death.
But
  Christ
    lives!

40

An Easter Prayer

Our Heavenly Father, we thank Thee for these springtime days when all the earth preaches a glad Easter gospel. As the great stone was rolled away from Christ's tomb, cold winter has been pushed aside by the angel of spring, and we behold a resurrection.

Crocuses, daffodils and tulips break forth from the earth. Buds and blossoms burst on limbs of shrubs and trees. The sad, dark soil becomes flushed with color as grasses awaken to the sun's tender touch. All that seemed dead comes alive.

Singing winds, chanting choruses of returning birds, and the laughter of children set free of winter wraps proclaim the glorious new life Thou hast given, and the promise of a more abundant life to come in springtime and summer days, now drawing near. For these earthly mementoes of the resurrection, we are grateful.

For Easter's reminder of Christ's victory over death we praise Thee. Now we know that, if the Easter gospel is true, the seal on the tomb is forever broken, on His tomb and ours, and death has lost its power to destroy our hope and joy.

Our Father, forbid that we ever treat Thy Christ as dead. Let us not embalm Him with rituals, bind Him with tight doctrines and lay Him away in churchly sacraments.

Let us remember that after Calvary, He showed Himself alive only to those who truly loved Him, and only by loving Him can we ever know the power of His resurrection. Then let us love Him!

Let us gladly claim His resurrection, that His presence may companion all our days, that His example may be the living center of all of our thinking and acting, and His love may govern our behavior toward all Thy children.

For our beloved dead who live with Thee, we thank Thee. When we remember Easter, we cannot weep in bitter anguish beside a loved one's grave, for Easter truth mixes gladness with sorrow. We thank Thee for the better life dear ones inherit, for the fuller wisdom they now know, for the greater joys and broader fellowships they experience, and that they are now nearer Thee than ties of earth ever allow. For faith that triumphs over grief, for trust in Thee that illumines loneliness and makes rainbows of our tears, we praise Thee.

We thank Thee for the change the Easter hope makes in all our days. Through Easter, like a door open heavenward, we see light, and we rejoice. Through Easter we know that if death is the end, it is only the end of our earthly limitations, the end of our infirmities and our abysmal ignorance of things eternal. Death is the end of the worst and the beginning of the best.

Through Easter we see that even the most awful tragedy, like Calvary, is made by Thee into ultimate triumph. Through Easter we know that earth's temporary victories, like that of Roman nails, are final defeats, and earth's seeming defeats are often Thy mighty victories.

Our Father, let us look at all of life in the clear light of Easter day, valuing most highly those things that death cannot corrode or snatch from us.

Let the full circle of our days have its center in Thee and be perfected by holding to Thy purpose for us, as was so of Christ, who came from Thee and returned to Thee.

Let us ever remember that Easter belongs to Calvary and beyond Black Friday waits Thy glad surprise, as surely as springtime waits beyond the bleakest winter, so that even the harshest disappointment cannot rob us of hope.

Thus may the truth, beauty and goodness of Easter touch all our tomorrows, and may we live all our days in the glory of that morning.

In Christ's name. *Amen.*

41

Lights Across the Bay

For several years our family lived on the shores of one of America's loveliest lakes, Michigan's Lake Charlevoix. Our home was only a few miles across the bay from the city of Charlevoix where I was pastor of a church. A variety of routes led to our home, and visitors from far away often came to see us by a road that missed the little city; thus they sometimes remained total strangers to Charlevoix. At night these guests would look from our living-room windows across the blue silences of the bay to the town we loved and remark how near and friendly the lights across the bay made Charlevoix seem to them. It always interested us to hear them try to describe the town by the few clues they could point to from the vantage point of our house. They guessed at the size of the city and its population. From its position on the lake shore they thought it must be a beautiful town to live in. Some surmised it might have a fishing industry, and others supposed (and rightly so) that it was a resort town, where people from across the nation would come for rest and relaxation.

From our dwelling upon the opposite shore our visitors could not see the small details of Charlevoix, such as the architecture of houses and people walking on the streets, but by seeing the lights across the bay they beheld enough to convince them that the city was a place of homes and people and fellowship.

Any attempt made by the children of earth to describe in detail the nature of heaven is doomed to failure. We have not been there. And even those who have lived closest to God, the saints and Christ Himself, have not tried to describe Heaven in great detail. Nevertheless, the question of what the Hereafter is like has always haunted the minds of men. As we look across the great quietness between here and there we try to guess. Are there any "lights across the bay" that will give us valid clues to what we may expect?

When Jesus spoke to His disciples concerning life beyond the grave, He gave them no detailed travelogue describing the geography, architecture, climate, or customs of Heaven. Instead

He simply said, "In my Father's house are many mansions: if it were not so I would have told you. I go to prepare a place for you." That is not a full description, but it is enough; it tells us all we really need to know. It indicates that our Eternal Home is spacious, and not a cramped little place, not some sort of a one-room apartment with room only for Him and you and me and those who see things precisely our way. One translation puts it, "In my Father's home are many rooms." Room for all nations, all races, room for many viewpoints and interpretations! Many rooms in the Father's house! That is a glimpse, a kind of beautiful intimation and an inference drawn from our own experience with rooms and space. No details, but a splendid clue — like lights across the bay.

Moreover, said Jesus, the life beyond this life is a place such as He could prepare; "I go to prepare a place for you." It is to His liking, and he loved companionship, conversation and service to human need. Heaven, then, must be adapted to human need — for the finest, richest expression of our best selves. If you want to know what the Hereafter is like for those who love God, simply ask yourself, "In the light of all I know about Jesus Christ, what kind of a place would he prepare?" All that we know about Him will give us valid clues.

There is another clue in the Gospels as to what God's children can expect to find in the Eternal Home. We discover one hint of Heaven in Saint Matthew's story of the first Easter morning. Matthew describes a scene of mixed sorrow and joy, tragedy and triumph. Mary Magdalene and the "other Mary" come to the tomb heartbroken. To their bewilderment they find the sepulchre open, and a heavenly messenger announces the glad news that death and the grave have been powerless to hold Jesus, "He is not here; for He is risen." Then the two Marys are instructed to go quickly and tell His disciples that He has gone before them into Galilee, where they will see Him.

As the women joyfully run from the tomb they meet Jesus, who greets them, "All hail!" The original Greek word used here, "chairete," is difficult to render into English. The Basic New Testament renders it "Be glad." Another translation is "Rejoice!" Still another translation interprets its meaning to be "All is well!" The original Greek expression was a commonplace greeting given when friend met friend, but in the context of the events of Black Friday and Easter the greeting has rare signifi-

133

cance. Nothing worse could happen to Jesus' body than what occurred on Calvary! He was shamefully executed as a common criminal and died a slow, torturous, agonizing death. The worst event that the disciples could conceive of had happened to them: they had lost Him, so it seemed — lost their dearest Friend, Teacher, Leader, Savior, and thus they had lost hope.

But now, three days after that hope-smashing event, Christ appears to them again, visibly and unmistakably, so that they are positive that death and the tomb have no power over Him. And He greets them, "Rejoice! All is well!" Coming from one

who had suffered what Christ had been through, those words
are more than a greeting. They are a report! It is not a *detailed*
description of what death means to God's own. It is a simple
summary of what death means to Him. After the most horrible
death conceivable, still Jesus can say, "Rejoice! All is well!"

For those who have lost dear ones lately, for those whose
hearts are heavy with fresh grief, that is good news indeed.
Christ's simple report concerning the death of God's children
may not tell us all we would like, but it tells us all we need
to know. "All is well" with them.

For those who love God, but fear death, Christ's Easter report is exciting, glorious, good news. Judged by the Resurrection Day announcement, there is new adventure waiting just ahead, a new freedom from the prison of flesh. The One who confidently had told His disciples, "In my Father's house are many mansions" and "I go to prepare a place for you" has Himself died, and, after experiencing the ugliest of all possible deaths, He has reported, "All is well! Rejoice!" If Easter is a clue, a "light across the bay," then death for God's children is homegoing to the Father's house. Death is life's glad journey to a place of Christ's liking, especially fitted to meet the soul's needs.

"Death" is but the poor, dark, clumsy word we use to describe life's greatest adventure.

Early African converts to Christianity grasped this glad Easter gospel, and ever afterward they would correct Christian missionaries who spoke of their dear dead as departed. "No!" the Africans would say. "He has arrived." That is it exactly! Death is arrival; death is fulfillment. All other events are but way-stations on our journey Home.

42

Both Now and Forever

Reading the gospel story of the first Easter is like stepping out of a stuffy, windowless room into the cool, clean air of April. The Easter atmosphere is good and exhilarating for tired souls. It is a place to breathe deeply, to clear clogged emotions, to stretch a cramped mind, to refresh a lagging spirit.

Much of the time we live in a world of temporal, time-bound things, of perishables, such as houses that need constant repair, automobiles that wear out and break down, clothes that tear or become threadbare. But Easter, with its deathless dimensions, reminds us of imperishables.

We feel condemned to performing tasks that, when done, must

be done over again, such as dishwashing, bed making and laundry, bookkeeping, payment of taxes, lawn mowing and weeding, so that life seems like a spiraling in circles which never gets us anywhere. Then comes Easter, and we remember that we have a destiny toward which we travel; we are not on a sickening, circling merry-go-round that takes us nowhere. We are journeying homeward.

On the first Easter Christ's disciples shouted the good news, "He lives!" He is here among us. The life He lived before the crucifixion goes on and on everlastingly. Death had done its worst, but it was not enough. Christ's life was eternal and so was the Christlike life of His followers. Later, when Christians suffered beheading, stoning, crucifixion, burning at the stake and death from the attacks of lions in Roman arenas, they continued to believe that a Christlike life has no ending, and that for the faithful all tombs are sealed in vain.

So after the first Easter the followers of Christ consciously lived in two worlds at a time — dealing with the perishable things of earth, such as daily bread, clothes, houses, and bodies that wear out or sicken and die, and the imperishable things of heaven, such as fellowship with man and God, love of goodness, truth and beauty, and loyalty to the Highest.

Living in two worlds at once seems impossible to some people. Henry David Thoreau, the poet, philosopher and naturalist, during his last illness was asked by a friend concerning his faith in a hereafter. The New Englander replied, "One world at a time, brother, one world at a time." But Thoreau himself had not practiced his motto, for all his days he had lived in two worlds, the one of material, measurable, weighable, perishable things and the other of everlasting things.

The Easter truth is that we are not meant solely for the present moment, nor are we intended for heaven exclusively. Both earth and heaven are God's and have a place in His plan for us. We are meant for here as well as the hereafter. It was never intended that we love the hereafter and hate all that is here or that we escape from present opportunities to serve God and man by fleeing to fantasies of glories yet to come. Nor are we meant to merely *endure* this world with stiff upper lips while we are here. Eternal life is a glad quality of living that is ours both now and forever, if we will accept it.

Anyone who has lost a loved one and has reflected long and

tenderly upon the meaning of it can appreciate what the death, resurrection and disappearance of Christ into heaven must have meant to the disciples. Such an experience makes us aware that we are of two worlds and that the world beyond is as real to us as the earth on which we dwell. Although the death of someone dear is grievous to us, it bestows at least this one blessing: it blends the Now and the Forevermore; it brings the Hereafter closer to the Here. It makes Heaven homelike, bestowing upon the life beyond death a consoling and satisfying familiarity.

Home is *not* where we are, as any traveler knows. Where we are at any given moment may be a highway, an airplane, a depot, a motel room, a camping site. Home is where our loved ones are, and where our thoughts linger lovingly. When we have loved ones There as well as Here, we are at home in two worlds, the Future and the Present, in Heaven and on Earth.

In Kenya, South Africa, a gravestone marks the burial place of Lord Baden-Powell, founder of the Boy Scout movement. The grave marker is inscribed: "Lord Baden-Powell, Chief Scout of the World. Born February 22, 1856, died January 8th, 1941." Beneath the inscription there appears a symbol that many a Scout has cut into the bark of a tree or made in the dust of a woodland path. It is a circle with a dot in the center, which is Scout sign-language meaning "I have gone home."

Everlasting life may mean many things, but especially this: possessing eternal life means being at home and feeling at home with God, *both* now and forever.

43

More to Follow

Rowland Hill, famed English preacher of the late eighteenth and early nineteenth centuries, loved to tell of his wealthy parishioner who was particularly fond of a certain poor member of the parish, and sought to relieve the misery of his poverty.

Yet he wanted to keep his philanthropy secret. Finally he concluded he could best express his care through a friend. The rich man gave his friend five pounds (at that time worth close to twenty-five dollars) to pass along to the poor man, together with a note that read, "This is yours. Use it wisely. There is more to follow." After a short time, he sent another five pounds with a note: "More to follow." So, throughout the years the kind benefactor frequently sent a gift of money, always accompanied with the cheerful news, "More to follow."

Thus it is with God's goodness and mercy: it comes to us marked with the good news, "More to follow!"

Our awareness of the dependable continuity of God's goodness is highest at Easter-time. Remember the story of the first Easter? On the preceding Friday Christ, believed by His disciples to be the Savior of the World, was cruelly crucified and His followers, believing that was the end of Him, laid His dead body to rest in a tomb, dropped their broken hopes and shattered dreams and returned to their routine tasks. Then Easter dawned. When some who loved Him went to the tomb to anoint His body, they found Christ's grave-clothes empty, and a heavenly messenger announced, "He is risen. He is not here." Shortly after this Christ appeared to His disciples very much alive. The resurrection event transformed broken-spirited disciples into joyous, venturesome, bold preachers of glad tidings, who risked death at the hands of their persecutors as they told the world of what Christ meant to them.

The Easter story reveals that precisely when we think the goodness of God has been exhausted, there is more. When the cross on Calvary seems to have put an end to the life of Christ, and there can be no more satisfying fellowship with Him, there is more. When the curtain of life has dropped on life's drama right at the most tragic instant, and we moan, "That is the end! That is the whole story!" there is more. And the best is yet to come.

Early Christianity began celebrating Easter as the central event of the faith. Easter was the soul's proof of the heart's surmise that all tombs are sealed in vain; that death does not mark the end of a person. Death does not finish our fellowship with God, or with our loved ones. There is more to follow. Until the first Easter men carried their dead to the grave, grieving the end of them. But the early Christians astonished and bewildered

139

the world as they celebrated funerals with songs of triumph, for they were convinced their loved ones had reached a new beginning, and every death had its own Easter Day.

Easter, then, means more than churches crowded with people sporting new "Easter outfits." It means even more than glad choir anthems and lily-scented air. Easter is more than a day — more, even, than a great and glorious holy day. Easter is a faith. It is the faith that Christ, and the things of Christ, cannot be finished by a cross and by man's awful hand, for they have deathless dimensions.

Easter is the faith that in God's providence everything can be made to work for the best, ultimately, even the worst intentions of men. Even when men spike the hands of God's Chosen One to a cross, the cross becomes the symbol of man's reconciliation with God, and the first Easter shows that the most dismal defeat becomes final victory, packed with hope for all mankind. So, some anonymous poet has said,

> *Lift up your heads, ye sorrowing ones,*
> *and be ye glad of heart,*
> *For Calvary and Easter Day were just three days apart.*

One summer a guest minister who was filling a pulpit for a vacationing clergyman found a banner that had been used the previous Easter Sunday. Emblazoned across the banner in big, bold, bright letters was the glad news, "He is risen!" But since Easter the banner had been tucked away in the coal bin of the church.

The Easter gospel is not reserved for Easter Sunday alone, to be preached and sung then and to be hidden the rest of the year. It is a joyous, everyday gospel, meant to brighten all our hours and to crown all our days with splendor. We are the children of the Eternal, the Easter faith proclaims, and we are meant to be everlasting. God's goodness and mercy have blessed us thus far, and there is more to follow in this life and the next. And the best is yet to come.

Everyone needs a faith like that every day. And that everyday faith was meant for everyone.

44

A Good Mother

Mother is the first and best thing that happens to children. Before a child comes into the world, or is known by anyone save God, it is loved and held closely by Mother.

Through a mother's pain we were born; through a mother's tender care our infant life was sustained; and all our days were warmed because Mother fanned the flames of life.

Mother hurts when and where anyone else in her family hurts. She is that lady of compassion whose temperature rises to 103 degrees whenever her child's temperature exceeds 98.6.

Simply having children does not make mothers of women. But loving children makes women mothers. Mothers come in all sizes and shapes. Mothers are nicely, if oddly, proportioned. The lowliest mother has high ideals. The slenderest has wide interests. The tallest has a short memory for our faults and failures. And even the tiniest mother has a big heart.

Every mother is a business woman. Her business is producing honorable men and women from the raw materials that come to her at birth. A mother's business in life is holy. To be entrusted with impressionable, pliable lives still unmolded is sacred. It is a holy thing to be able to impress little ones with honesty, honor, love and loyalty. To be able to lift a life so high (or depress a life so low) is a sacred business. A mother is a sacred-business woman.

Some people in this world deserve little and get much, and some deserve much and get little. Mother pays little attention to what she deserves and to what she gets. She is too busy seeing what she can do for anyone who needs her. She is preoccupied making her todays into our tomorrows.

Mother makes every day a birthday of sorts, loading her family with gifts of understanding and forgiveness, appreciation, encouragement, comfort and devotion, all splendidly wrapped in kindly deeds.

Most mothers raise their children "by the book" — some by a child psychology book, or an emergency medicine book, or by comic books, or by bank books. The good mother always includes "the Good Book."

She's a genius at efficiency; when the children are small she not only gets everything done in a day, but gets everything done a dozen times over! Mother seldom has a chance to worry about what her children will be when they grow up. She's too busy chasing after them to see what they are up to now.

Mother is that gracious lady who has never learned to count — to count herself first, or to count herself in when it comes to enough pie, or ice cream or any of the rest of life's material advantages.

A good mother is the equal of a dozen school teachers, a small convention of clergymen, and a score of policemen and judges, all added together. A mother is a Jacquelyn-of-all-trades. She is a singer, whose hymns crooned at the cradle and sung at the ironing board and the kitchen sink will, like God's goodness and mercy, follow us all the days of our lives. She preaches sermons one can see, as well as hear, by the way she walks happily through our lives. (She is the only Bible some people of the neighborhood ever read.) She models, and womanhood looks good on her. She is an interpreter who knows the precise meaning of a baby's cry, a boy's anguished yelp, a daughter's sob or a husband's scowl, and she comes on the run with the exact answer.

Mother is a clever magician, adroitly changing life's heaviest drudgery into life's highest privilege, making ordinary sons look like heroes and transforming ordinary daughters into radiant angels by waving a word of praise. With a reassuring word she makes childhood worries disappear into thin air, and with a touch of her hand she changes a child's chaos to calmness. With her softly spoken prayer the air is cleared of anger and ill-will, and all our sin-soiled world seems bright and good again.

A skeptic once asked me why I believe in God. I fumbled for words, came up with a weak explanation, and tossed it aside in utter frustration. Then a mother walked through the room, carrying her little babe, and all I needed was to point a finger and say, "There!"

A good mother is the most convincing argument for God I've ever seen, for mothers don't just happen; mothers are Heaven-sent. Mothers are God's goodness wearing an apron, God's truth setting the table, God's beauty tenderly saying, "Goodnight, Dear. I'll see you in the morning."

45

Prayer for the Mothers of the World

O God, our Father, we thank Thee for those devoted women, our mothers, who, after Thee, were first among the influences that formed our lives; whose arms held us with a tenderness like Thine own; who, through childhood days, blessed us with encouragement, praise, wise counsel, kind looks and caring ways, with the shelter of their love and the protection of their prayers. We rejoice in those mothers who — through their own exemplary lives — made it easy to believe in Thee.

We thank Thee for every moment hallowed and every place made sacred by the dedicated love of mothers. With gratitude we recall their spoken prayers; their singing gladness for the good received from Thee and the world; their shy silence concerning services they rendered Thee and Thy children, with no intention of reward and no hope of praise.

With thanks to Thee we remember their compassion for the world's hurt and helpless; their righteous anger at oppression and all manner of injustice; their urgent haste in answering the cry of human need; their strength in bearing misunderstanding, ingratitude, disappointment and grief.

Give to all mothers the courage of clear and mighty convictions in these perplexing and troubled times, and steadiness in these days when the foundations of the world are shaken. When they are weary, refresh them with the vision of the good they have accomplished. When they are saddened by the waywardness of their children, fearing their teaching and example have

been in vain, remind them that no good a mother has done is ever lost in Thy world; its lasting influence is guaranteed by Thee.

Thou hast let mothers share with Thee the mystery of creation, entrusting them with the formation of little lives. May mothers also be given a generous share of Thy wisdom, so that the world's children may be nurtured in the ways of love, mutual concern and helpfulness, in ways of forgiveness and reconciliation that make for peace.

May mothers direct the next generation into paths of righteousness; its ambitions into worthy goals; its passions toward goodness, truth and beauty; its dedication to Thee and the things of Thy kingdom.

May mothers influence the future of the world by communicating the best Thou hast wrought within them to those around them. May they make of the home a school where the highest values of life are taught; a gallery where the beauties of life are hung before the minds of all who dwell there; a shelter where there is serenity and warmth of love, security and protection from the harshness of the world; a sanctuary, sanctified by prayer, where Thou art near and real, where tired souls are refreshed and inspiration for courageous living is constantly renewed.

Since the world's future will largely depend upon what the world's mothers are, make them in every way what Thou wouldst have them be, so that Thy kingdom at last may come, and Thy will be truly done, "on earth as it is in heaven." Thus may they be Thy happy partners in a new creation.

In the name of the Christ whom Thou entrusted to the care of a mother, who was first at His cradle, and last at His cross and always in His love. Amen.

46

How Is Everything at Home?

This miracle month of May calls us to be attentive to fundamental things. May speaks of essentials, of spring's plenty that overcomes winter's scarcity, of a creativeness which is greater than the world's destructiveness, of growth that conquers stagnation, of excitement that vanquishes boredom.

May is a month of a million births. This month the first fawns of spring will open wide eyes upon wonders spread lavishly around them. Coonlets and chunky woodchuck babies will first see the light of day. Nests are being built by our winged neighbors, and some eggs will be hatched before May merges into June. Already dandelions have flowered. Yellow and lavender violets and adder's-tongues bloom under our spreading beech trees.

Now quickens that process that is elemental to life on earth, photosynthesis. Our tallest trees and smallest plants of woodland and meadow drink deeply of spring sunlight and rain, and in each plant laboratory the light and water transform nutriments from soil and air into plant food. The plants in turn become nourishment for animals, and so life thrives because it is attentive to this fundamental thing, photosynthesis.

Maybe May is so heartening, bracing and refreshing because it turns our minds from the trivia that so often engage them to the essential elements that are the cosmic backing upon which we lean. And maybe we could restore joy to life on any day of any month if we would, for even a little while, become so attentive and appreciative of life's elemental blessings — available to us all — that we would forget to fret about the lack of luxurious nonessentials that are within the reach of only a few.

May is an appropriate month for the celebration of Mother's Day and to think of home, for home is one of life's fundamentals. It is there we learn to laugh and weep and discover what is worthy of our laughter and tears. There, too, we learn to love good and hate evil to the measure that parents love and hate and according to their standards of values.

In the home we learn unselfishness from that woman, called "Mother," who pretends she doesn't care much for pie when she finds there are only four pieces to serve five people. We catch a contagious concern for the sick and the hurt from that good soul whose temperature soars to 104 degrees whenever her child's temperature reaches 100.

Home is a place of heart-keeping more than house-keeping. It is a place for building mutual respect, self-confidence and confidence in others, enduring affection, fidelity to high principles, hopes and dreams.

A good home is the best place on earth to learn patience and how to get along with other people, a lesson all people of all nations desperately need in our time. It is here, in the home, where people of different sexes, ages and interests abide together, that we learn that *differences need make no difference* in our care for each other.

Home is the one place where the world's greatest are ordinary people, where ordinary people receive extraordinary attention and affection, and where every nobody is really somebody. Mother sees to that!

A few weeks ago, when we celebrated Good Friday, we read again from John's Gospel the moving expression, "There stood by the cross of Jesus his mother." Even a cross of execution could not separate Christ from His mother.

In our worst hours and in our best the influences of mother and home are always with us. Thus, every day is unavoidably Mother's Day.

47

Everything Leaves Its Mark

Everything tends to leave its mark as it passes through the world.

Animals do. Only a small percentage of the creatures living in field and forest are seen by man. Still, we know of the presence of many others, for each one leaves some signs of itself as it moves about or rests.

An animal's feeding habits make a trail of hints and clues as to what the creature is like, and what it has been doing. Deer browsing on red maple or poplar shoots or the boughs of white cedar leave tell-tale ragged edges on the twigs where they have fed, while cottontail rabbits and snowshoe hares clip off the twigs as neatly as if they had been cut with a razor blade. (This is because deer, like cattle, have no front teeth on the upper jaw, and therefore cannot make a clean cut, while rabbits and hares have sharp incisors on both jaws.)

Bears rip at rotting logs, searching for grubs and insects and whitefooted mice. Squirrels indicate food preferences by the green cones, terminal twigs, buds and the nuts they cut from trees.

Hair on barbed wire fences, logs, stumps and rubbing posts show which animals have passed that way. Mud wallows, dusting places and beds show where creatures have bathed, frolicked or rested, and tell a bit about their size, weight and their habits.

Tracks of shore birds ring our Meadow's Edge Pond and embroider the banks of the brook that skips past our library door. And the tracks tell much about the bird's size, feeding habits, and whether or not its feet are webbed and adapted to swimming.

Many of the world's lakes and ponds are the "tracks" left by shifting in the earth's crust; or by volcanic action that left craters that filled with water; or by the action of glaciers; or by landslides that blocked off valleys, forming natural dams; or by beavers building dams across streams. The earth is covered by clues of events that transpired thousands of years ago.

Much modern crime detection is based upon the assumption

that everyone leaves behind him some signs of what he is like and what he has been doing. Soil samples taken from his tracks, lint left by his clothes, bits of hair, dust, lipstick on a drinking glass, or a smudge of grease or oil from a working glove, a fleck of blood, or a scrap of handwriting, footprints and fingerprints all serve to show what he has been up to, and what he is like.

One of the glories and tragedies of the home is that each person goes out into the world stamped with the influences of family living. Each person in the family leaves his mark on every other person. This is a splendid fact when the home has splendor, when it is distinguished by good humor and cheer, joy, self-control, patience, mutual respect, reverence for the Eternal and commitment to Christ. But it is a tragic fact when the home is seared and scarred by smoldering hostility, irritability, fault-finding, constant bickering and quarreling grudgefulness. These leave imprints upon all members of the family, who in turn influence the immediate community and the world. Better homes mean a better world.

We are either lamplighters or arsonists. We take from our homes and spread all around us either lights that illumine and give hope, or flames that destroy. One way or the other, wherever we go, we shall leave signs of what we are and the kind of homes from which we come.

On the banks of the James River stands a tombstone erected by a pioneer in tender memory of his wife who followed him from England to America. The inscription reads, "She touched the soil of Virginia with her little foot and the wilderness became a home." Nothing lovelier could be said of any of us than that we made this wild world homelike for someone by our love and influence. Two things we know about that woman. The world became a bit better because she lived here for a while. And she left a touch of beauty here, because someone had first blessed her life with a similar influence for good.

Such is the sequence of Christian experience: it is like the game "Pass It On," which we played as children. Such objects as a ball, a pencil, a bell or a hat were passed down two lines of contestants to see which group could get the objects through the line most quickly without dropping one of them. Each person was responsible for passing on whatever treasure came into his hands.

So with life. We all receive. For better or worse, we all give.

A Christian is responsible for passing on the best that God has given him through others.

This is the way the Gospel and the Church have survived. In this way God gets His work done.

This is one way we "count" and make a difference for good in God's world.

Memorial Day

48

A Well-Used Memory
Is a Holy Thing

A well-used memory is a holy thing. It is an instrument for bringing the best hours and influences of the past into the present to bless "the here-and-now" and to inspire noble conduct.

Dr. Edward C. Rosenow, known throughout the world as one of the greatest bacteriologists, decided, while still a small boy, to become a doctor. What prompted this early decision? A lighted face influenced his choice. Rosenow grew up on a farm in an isolated area of Wisconsin. One night Edward's brother became critically ill and the lad's parents were frightened and in despair because the nearest doctor lived many miles away. But the physician was sent for, and he came as quickly as possible.

Little Edward followed the doctor into the room where his

brother lay near death. Hiding behind a big chair, Edward watched in awe as the physician ministered to the sick child. Soon the doctor turned to the parents and declared, "Have no fear. The boy will get well." At this glad news the parents' faces brightened in a way Edward could never forget.

At that moment, Dr. Rosenow later testified, he decided that the one thing he wanted most in the world was to do the things that would cause such a light of joy and gratitude to illumine the faces of people. All of Edward Rosenow's days, and the lives of thousands of his patients, were blessed because of that sacred memory. Doctor Rosenow's experience illustrates what Dostoevsky once said, "You must know that there is nothing higher and stronger and more wholesome and good for life than some good memory, especially a memory of childhood."

Individually, nationally and culturally we are rich or poor according to the abundance of good things we have stored in our memories. Our present civilization would be little or nothing if it were not for memories. Memory makes all learning possible; without it we would all need to begin each day as empty of knowledge as was the first infant born on earth. Without memory no lessons from the past could be passed on to us. The great reformers, prophets, and evangelists have always insisted that they were but reminding men of precious truths that had been forgotten.

Christmas, Easter, and all other holidays consist largely of the celebration of lovely and holy things we hold in our memory. Especially is this so of the holiday millions of Americans celebrate at the end of May. Memorial Day, otherwise known as Decoration Day, is a special time many Americans set aside for gratefully remembering how much their dear dead have meant to them.

Now, when this holy time of special recollection returns, we gratefully recall names, faces, voices, gestures, sacrifices, and happy moments we have known in years that have gone. Some of these dear ones abruptly left their homes to die bravely on far-off battle fields, on the high seas, or in the air for a cause they believed to be just. Their sacrifices were great and spectacular. Others lived quietly in our midst saying the right word, the encouraging, heartening word, performing the gracious deeds so that life was richer, sweeter because they had been among us. We remember them all with gratitude.

151

How can we make Memorial Day more meaningful? George Gilbert Murray, the British classical scholar and longtime professor of Oxford University, said that during the First World War he walked around the quadrangles at Oxford, heavy in spirit because he remembered that brave men were dying for him in France. On Memorial Day, and every other day of the year, all sensitive souls have memories enriched by thoughts of those who have sacrificed, and suffered anguishing toil, pain and death that we might live.

We can never repay them. Yet we can demonstrate gratitude. The one gift we can all give to the dead is to be better people because they once lived among us. A monumental life lived in their memory is better than any monumental stone we can erect on their graves.

Summertime Holiday

49

In the Hand of God

The founding of our government was an exciting, dangerous and highly uncertain adventure. At first it appeared well-nigh impossible to unite the colonies. An Englishman who visited these shores in 1760 wrote his impressions: "Fire and water are not more heterogeneous than the different colonies in North America. Nothing can exceed the jealousy which they possess in regard to each other. The inhabitants of Pennsylvania and New York have an inexhaustible source of animosity in their jealousy for the trade of the Jerseys. Massachusetts Bay and Rhode Island are not less interested in that of Connecticut. Even the limits and boundaries of each colony are a constant source of litigation. In short, such is the difference of character, of manners, of religion, of interest in the different colonies that I think, if I am not wholly ignorant of the human mind, were they left to themselves, there would soon be a civil war from one end of the continent to the other." It appeared the colonies did not have the ghost of a chance of forming an independent nation of free colonies united into a strong nation.

An old bellringer, who had been instructed to remain within calling distance at Constitutional Hall so that he could begin ringing the Liberty Bell as soon as the Declaration of Independence had been adopted by the Convention, was most pessimistic. He went around shaking his head and muttering hopelessly, "They'll never do it! They'll never do it!"

There were times when it appeared the bellringer was right. The fifty-five men who had met to prepare a constitution could not agree on the basic elements of the future government. Although they met nearly every day for almost five weeks, they made little progress. On the last morning of the fifth week there was more heated debate, but still no decisions were made. Some were in favor of adjournment and abandonment of any plan for

155

a federal union of the colonies. A United States of America did not have a chance.

Then Benjamin Franklin arose. He addressed the chairman: "Mr. President, the small progress we have made after four or five weeks' close attention and continual reasonings with each other our different sentiments on almost every question, several of the last producing as many 'Noes' as 'Ayes,' is methinks a melancholy proof of the imperfection of the human understanding. . . .

"In this situation of this assembly, groping as it were, in the dark, to find political truth, and scarce able to distinguish it when presented to us, how has it happened, sir, that we have not hitherto once thought of humbly applying to the Father of Lights to illuminate our understanding? We have been assured, sir, in the Sacred Writings that 'except the Lord build the house, they labor in vain that build it.' I therefore beg to move that henceforth prayers, imploring the assistance of Heaven and its blessings on our deliberations, be held in this assembly every morning before we proceed to business. . . ." From that time on the Convention made progress.

On another day during the hard debates and harsh disagreements that characterized the Constitutional Convention, George Washington arose and said to the delegates: "It is too probable that no plan we propose will be adopted. Perhaps another dreadful conflict is to be sustained. If to please the people we offer what we ourselves disapprove, how can we afterwards defend our work? Let us raise a standard to which the honest can repair. *The event is in the hand of God.*"

We cannot account for America without considering its religious roots. Its earliest leaders were men whose religious faith overcame prevailing pessimism. A clergyman, the Reverend John Witherspoon, who was president of the College of New Jersey, was a signer of the Declaration of Independence. The patriotic hymn "My Country 'Tis of Thee" was written in 1832 by a Baptist minister, the Reverend Samuel Francis Smith. Another Baptist clergyman, the Reverend Francis Bellamy, authored the "Pledge of Allegiance to the Flag" in 1892. So, while at the beginning America didn't seem to have "the ghost of a chance" of being born or surviving, the United States of America was established and has been sustained by such men of faith.

156

Americans fought and died to free this country from the shackles that stretched across the sea, but the nation was not built upon a foundation of swords, muskets and cannon.

America was rich in material resources, in land, forests, crops and gold, but America's true foundation is not material wealth.

Americans have an abundance of patriotic pride and a love for American institutions, anthems and flag, but America's foundations are not in patriotic sentiment.

The strength of America now, as at its beginning, is in our trust that we have "the assistance of Heaven and its blessings" in doing the right, and that our destiny is "in the hand of God."

And just as our foundations are spiritual, so our *chief problem* now is spiritual. In 1876 the English scientist, Thomas Huxley, visited the United States to lecture at Johns Hopkins University. In his address he said, "I cannot say that I am in the slightest degree impressed by your bigness or your material resources as such. Size is not grandeur, territory does not make a nation. The great issue, about which hangs a true sublimity and the terror of overhanging fate, is 'What are you going to do with these things?'"

This is still the big question, and it is a spiritual one: "Agreed that America has the world's greatest wealth and power, what will Americans do with these things?"

50

An American Prays for His Country

God of our fathers, Father of all mankind, beneath whose guiding hand our forebears crossed the seas and established a great nation: we thank Thee for this land we love; for far-flung, lavish beauties of forests, mountains, plains and waters; for an abundance of natural wealth that flows from the rich earth; for fertile fields that feed a hungry world; for industries and trades that toil to meet the world's growing needs.

We praise Thee for those who, in generations past, have taken the pains and dared to die to establish and preserve our nation and its liberties. For this nation's spirit we thank Thee, Father: for freedom's soil beneath our feet and freedom's air to breathe; for free expression of religious faith, unfettered by the state; for churches where the glad Gospel of Thy grace is freely preached; for national shrines that remind us of past greatness, present duties and future opportunities; for the joyous welcome this land has extended and still holds forth to the freedom-hungry and downtrodden who seek these shores. Accept our thanks, O God, for the best of man's past brought here by native people of all parts of the world. For every good thing now woven into the beauty and strength of this good land; for the grandeur of the past, the challenge of these hours, and for the hope of the tomorrow we thank Thee, O God.

O Lord, forgive us where we have taken for granted, as our just due, the blessings of our country, simply because they have come so easily to most of us. Where in time of peace we have forgotten the hardships endured and the sacrifices made in time of war for our sakes, where in our comforts we have not remembered those who have made our safety possible, pardon us. If we have lost sight of the real America and have mistaken self-righteousness for pursuit of the right, or have confused conformity with unity, or self-justification with justice, or force with moral strength, forgive us. If we have been smug and complacent with material advantages, or have allowed ourselves to become softened by our comforts, or have sought ease rather than adventure, or have been more concerned about rights than we have about duties, forgive.

O God, Ruler of all the earth, hear our prayer for our homeland that it may be always a blessing to the world. While we pray Thou wilt guard our shores from every foe, we also beseech Thee that Thou wilt protect us from enemies within. Save us from passions of fear and wrath that blind men to reason and stifle wisdom. Spare us from that arrogance that is so often the companion of bigness, wealth and power.

Let us never forget the meaning of America or the qualities of heroic patience and endurance that have distinguished our past and that the future will demand. Make us strong to withstand sudden shock and disappointment and to suffer a prolonged crisis. Grant us the daring and willingness to be misunderstood and criticized and to be rebuffed in our role of serving world need. Grant us the rugged courage to be critical of ourselves, of our motives and policies, without rancor against those citizens who differ from our views. Let government always be the good and faithful servant of all our people, working for the welfare of all, and never an oppressive master.

We pray that America may be prepared for the decisive days that lie just ahead. Clarify and sharpen the vision and thinking of our leaders and make them faithful servants of Thy people's needs and of Thy purposes, eager to know and glad to do Thy holy will. May generosity of thought and conduct distinguish us in our dealings with each other and with those who live beyond our borders. May we help make the world safe for differences of opinion.

Spare us from undue pride in material greatness. We pray that not only harvests and herds, factories and mills, barns and warehouses, laboratories of science, schools and colleges may multiply and national wealth may prosper, but that our spiritual health may improve and the soul of America may grow. Temper our great power with a still greater compassion and with undiscourageable goodwill so that we may not flaunt our strength like a boasting giant but bend in tenderness and helpfulness, like a Good Samaritan, over a stricken and wounded world.

Lord of all nations, all the good we desire for this land we love we ask for all nations and all men everywhere. Hasten the day when all the world will be cleansed of hatred and war, when all the sons and daughters of earth are united in love and peace as children of one Father, when every human life is held sacred by all other souls, and every nation is a Holy Land. Through Jesus Christ, our Lord. *Amen.*

Some Very Special Days

Birthday

51

Best Wishes

For two or three generations now, "wishful thinking" has been a disagreeable expression, denoting some slight ailment of mind and spirit. While the diagnosis is not as disturbing as outright mental disease, wishful thinking has been given a sickish cast, a sort of "sniffles of the psyche."

A portion of this reputation is deserved. At its worst, wishful thinking represents self-deception for purposes of maintaining self-respect, such as the use of ingenious excuses, or coaxing oneself to believe that an evil deed "won't count this time," or any other device that makes foolish or immoral conduct seem justified. We wish the act *could* be justified. Then we talk ourselves into believing it is a blameless act. For example, a man feels he ought to be at his work, which is urgent, or it is Sunday morning, and he feels he should be at worship. But he wishes he were on the golf course instead. So he tells himself that he desperately needs physical exercise, and then he will be able to work more efficiently. Or he persuades himself that he can go to church on rainy Sundays and golf on sunshiny Sundays. (As if the soul needs strengthening and communion with God only when skies are heavy!)

Or a little girl is given twenty-five cents to take to church "to give to God." But she wishes she could buy an ice-cream soda instead. She stops at the drugstore on the way to church and buys the soda. Later she explains to her parents, "I gave the quarter to the soda-fountain man, and *he* can give it to God!" It *sounds* reasonable, doesn't it?

When wrongly employed, wishful thinking is a device for pursuing any course of action we desire, while inventing explanations which *seem* justified. It is naked self-deception. Mob lynchings are perpetrated because "the law is too slow," or "to protect the virtue of our women," or "to render justice," but never admittedly "because we are cruel animals, covered with a thin

161

veneer of civilization that comes off under pressure." Nations make war, persuading themselves that their motives are pure and their cause is just. Has any modern nation ever warred against another, giving as its reason, "because we are afraid of our neighbors and hope to kill them before they kill us," or "because we are greedy," or "because we are barbarians at heart"?

Wishful thinking deceives the self and escapes stern realities by taking refuge in daydreams, fictions and fabrications.

But wishful thinking is also one of the most glorious activities of the mind of man, when it is rightly used. Little good is accomplished in this world until it is first wished for, deeply desired. The great explorations were launched and the epochal discoveries were made following much wishful thinking. Advances in medical science have followed a profound wish that man's sufferings could be eased and his diseases cured. The glad Gospel of God's forgiving love and saving grace has been preached when men who have experienced it have wished to share the good news with others.

My mind has been dwelling on wishful thinking since the arrival of birthday greeting cards in this morning's mail bearing messages of "Best wishes!" and

Happy Birthday!
And may it bring to you
The best in everything.
But words alone cannot express
All that's wished for your happiness!

— and similar expressions of wishful thinking. At birthday time, on wedding occasions and wedding anniversaries, at Christmas and New Year's, when we are ill or when we are leaving on a long voyage, we receive greeting cards and letters that include the salute "Best wishes!" We also send such greetings. What do we mean when we wish another person "the best"?

I am unsure as to all that others have in mind when they send me "best wishes," but here, in capsule form, are some of the values I include when I wish you and others the best.

Since quality of life comes from the soul's hunger and the mind's probing, may you suffer enough divine discontent to keep you ever pushing forward.

May you have the rare happiness of an undistracted, wholehearted journey toward a goal you believe is God's plan for your life.

May you be given strength to reject the *good* while searching for the *best*.

When you stumble and fall, may you always fall forward, toward your goal.

May you enjoy the richness of soul that is the result of seeing that your spiritual income always exceeds your expenditures.

May you enjoy the exciting fun of keeping company with the great and riding on the shoulders of giants. Through good reading and quiet contemplation you can be carried high on the thoughts of the best men of all time, and — through the Gospels — have fellowship with the mind of Christ Himself. Aware that those who can read and do not are as mentally poor as those who cannot read at all, may you read the best, thus spending hours with the towering souls of all ages.

As a tree continues to grow to its dying day, may you grow in wisdom and spirit as long as you live.

May you always possess your possessions; may they never possess you.

May you always have the wisdom and strength to say "No" to some things so that you can say "Yes" to other important things.

May you know the joys of fellowship with those you love, who return your love, and with those who love the things you love, *to* whom you look with admiration and trust and *with* whom you look toward the same purposes and goals. May you know the happiness that multiplies as you divide it with others.

Since much of the good life consists of fellowship through communication between ourselves and others, may you be blessed with the high art of conversation, which is not only that of "catching on" but letting go, and which consists of saying the right thing in the right place and leaving unsaid the wrong thing at the tempting moment.

If you cannot be great in big ways and big places, may you be great in small ways and common places. And greatness means this above all else, being far more kind than those around you deserve.

May you be free of the perils of playing God, feeling responsible for running the entire universe. Yet, may you know the wholesome responsibility of carrying your own burdens — and sometimes those of your fellowmen — cheerfully.

May you be blessed with health and with the laughter that is God's good medicine for all men.

May you be free from too much concern about success, which is one of this world's chief idols. May you have the steadying confidence that when you have, by God's grace, done the best that is in you, you can leave the rest to Him, and to time, to determine its value.

May you find the changeless, steady values in a changeful and unsteady world, and the Eternal amidst matters that erode and vanish.

May you be blessed with a memory that is both splendid and poor; splendid in its remembrance of kindnesses you have received from God and man, and often forgetful of the benefits you have conferred on others.

May life not be too stormy, yet may you have enough clouds in your sky to make breathtaking dawns and beautiful sunsets.

No matter what the eroding years may do to your face and figure, may you find an answer to the wise petition of Socrates, "I pray thee, O God, that I may be beautiful within."

Finally, may you have the joyful satisfaction of making a difference for good wherever you go. Abraham Lincoln wistfully said, "Die when I may, I want it said of me by those who knew me best, that I always plucked a thistle and planted a flower where I thought a flower would grow." May the world have fewer thistles and more flowers because you are here for awhile.

164

52

A Prayer When a Child Is Born

O God, the Source from which we all have come, we thank Thee for this sign that Thou art not discouraged with the world: a child has been born. We praise Thee for every new-born babe, for every new commingling of the Divine with our dust, and especially for this child, this bright little horizon where earth and Heaven meet.

❋ ❋ ❋

Bless him this day and all his days. In his infancy may he be quietly aware of the love that nurtures and shelters him. Let each day move him from helpless babyhood toward helpful manhood. May the highest ideals and noblest purposes be transplanted from his parents' hearts and minds to his fertile character; there may they grow and be fruitful.

❋ ❋ ❋

Grant him a curious and appreciative interest in the world around him, a zest for life, and a passion for goodness. Give him both grace of bearing and beauty in the inner man. Stretch his mind and heart to make room for Thee and a place for all mankind, and let him become like the Boy of Nazareth who "increased in wisdom and stature, and in favor with God and man."
In His name. *Amen.*

53

The Meaning of Marriage

(A Letter to Newlyweds on Their Wedding Day)

So you have reached your wedding day at last!

Today the dear dream comes true. Now the sacred, final word is spoken. From this glad hour the world will know you belong to each other forever.

Now begins the life-long miracle, daily renewed — discovering the wonders that abide in another's heart and mind. Today begins the sharing of a single life and destiny, as the solemn, beautiful old ritual phrases it, "for better, for worse, for richer, for poorer, in sickness and in health, 'til death do us part." From this blessed day the two streams of your existence will mingle and flow as one, with double their former force.

WHAT IS THIS NEW AND SACRED RELATIONSHIP YOU BEGIN TODAY?

Marriage is reaching out for the completion and fulfillment in another that no one can find in oneself. It is love carried to the

166

highest degree, just short of your love for God and God's love for you. Married love is a life-long conversation that seems far too short, where each tells the other by words, by glances and by deeds that you continue to care, that you understand or will try to understand, that your loyalty and love will never fail when it is needed.

Married love is the *habit* of the tender look, the gentle word, the thoughtful deed and the unexpected kindness that go far beyond the demands of duty and far exceed the vows taken today.

Marriage is a *revelation*, for it is the greatest test of character ever devised. It offers more opportunities for blundering or success, for selfishness or kindly consideration, for fretfulness or patience, for foolishness or wisdom, for severity or tenderness, than any other situation in life. Marriage, like no other relationship, discloses what we are. Beginning this day, you will be exposed to the clearest possible revelation of the flaws and beauty, the little weaknesses and the glorious strength of manhood and womanhood.

But marriage is more, far more, than a revelation. Marriage is *a transformation*. It makes one person of two people. It enlarges your spirit, broadening and deepening your soul, making more room in you for sadness and joy, for tears and laughter, for discord and harmony, sacrifice and gain, struggle and success, for self-interest, concern for others and love for God. Marriage is an enlargement of life. Life will be more full now than ever before, since you belong to each other. Rejoice in life's fullness.

WHEN IS MARRIAGE MOST HAPPY?

Golden rings do not make a marriage. Neither do civil licenses, or ministers, or altars, or lovely candlelit ceremonies. What, then, are the essentials of a happy, satisfying, enduring marriage?

Your wedding life will be happy if it is a deep and abiding commitment, composed of faith and confidence in each other and mutual respect.

Remember, always, your deep indebtedness to each other, for a good marriage is one in which each of you obtains from the other more than either of you can ever hope to repay.

When a married person speaks of his spouse as his "better half" he is careless of his fractions. Your partner in marriage will always be more than half your joy, more than half your concern in life, more than half of your enthusiasms, more than half your plans for the future.

Married love does not mean thinking *alike* on all matters, but it does mean thinking *together* about important matters.

Your differences will never matter as much as indifference. Your care for each other will grow as your concern for what each other thinks and feels and desires is strengthened.

It is as important that you grow in love as it was that you fall in love. It is as urgent that your love mature and ripen as it was that it bud and blossom. Therefore, encourage love's fulfillment. Shelter it from harsh words and from sullen silences. Warm it with increasing care for one another's comfort, pleasure and peace. Let increasing tenderness enrich its roots and a climate of nourishing goodwill draw forth its unfolding goodness.

Most men and women are "appreciated into marriage." Love is not really blind, but sees possibilities, virtues and values easily missed by unloving eyes; love notices and praises what the world overlooks. Be generous in your use of honest praise. Appreciation is bread, butter, meat and milk for the soul. At all costs, keep your appreciations alive and active. They have brought you together. They are God-given graces that will draw you ever closer to each other.

Miles of distance can never separate two who truly love each other, and confinement in one room can never bring two together if love is not there. Reinforce your love by joining more and more of your interests so that the union performed on your wedding day may be but the beginning of a fuller mingling of hearts and minds. Let marriage be rooted in companionship. May your wedding not end a beautiful friendship, but enrich, broaden and deepen it.

While a marriage may be made in Heaven, it must be lived on earth. While a wedding may take place at an altar, it finds its meaning, as well, in the kitchen, living room, bedroom, backyard, at grocery stores, at work, at play and at worship. While marriage has to do with exchange of rings, it has even more to do with exchange of gentle glances, tender words, confidences and trust.

Since many of your hours together will be spent in conversation, give daily attention to a growing richness of your minds, so that your interest in what is said by one another may be as intense on the fiftieth anniversary of this glad day as it was on the night of your engagement.

Regardless of the style of your *house*, let the style of your *home* be split level, where earth and Heaven meet. May the home within your house have a foundation of lasting loyalty. May it possess high ideals. May it be well lighted by truth, fragrant with fairness, airy with delight, gaiety, laughter, and dreams of a bright future. Let it have doors that shut out strife and shut in an abundance of security and contentment. May it have windows where the light of love shines out upon a world that is often dark, sorely needing the light you have to give. May the right temperature in your home be maintained by warm hearts.

If children come to bless your days, and pray Heaven they may, may there be time for toys and games and romping on the floor, time for table grace and bedside prayers.

May there always be a welcome at your door, and may you always want to run the last steps homeward.

On this day when you are bound together for life, begin to speak the language of love, the holiest word of which is "ours." ("Ours" is the sacred translation of the old word "my" that you used so often in former days.) Now your conversation will be hallowed by the new word, sprinkled, like holy water, everywhere — "Our life together," "our home," "our plans," "our vacation," "our children," "our church," "our Father which art in heaven." May the word "my" fade away and the holy word "our" find increasing use and meaning in your lives.

Finally, remember that a happy marriage is not where two are joined as partners, but three: you, your beloved and your God. You will need God even more than you need each other, not simply in keeping holy vows but in being what you want to be. And success in marriage involves far more than finding the right person. It is mostly a matter of *being* the right person.

God bless your marriage, that it may not shackle you, but that it may liberate you. If a good marriage is ever a burden, it is such a weight as a sail is to a ship and as wings are to a bird. Marriage fulfills.

God's blessing binds you now with a strength the law does not possess. You belonged to God long before you belonged to each other. Therefore, remember God, His interest in your life together, His claims upon you, His love which encompasses all human loves, as the sea receives at last all earth's flowing waters.

My best wishes, my blessings and my prayers for your lasting happiness are with you now and always.

Affectionately yours,
Harold E. Kohn

54

Thanks for the Silences

HEAVENLY FATHER,
I THANK THEE
FOR
THE
BEAUTIFUL,
UNDERSTOOD SILENCES
OF
A HAPPY MARRIAGE,
FOR
EVERY MOMENT
TOO
DEEP
FOR WORDS.

AMEN

About the Author

HAROLD E. KOHN

A man of wide-ranging interests and talents, Harold Kohn has effectively woven them into a career devoted to helping others. Dr. Kohn is a clergyman (most recently the minister of the First Congregational Church, Charlevoix, Michigan, and now retired because of ill health); a counsellor of the troubled; a writer on nature, psychology, philosophy, and religion; the author of the following books: *Feeling Low? Through the Valley, Pathways to Understanding, Thoughts Afield, Reflections, A Touch of Greatness, Adventures in Insight, The Tinsel and the Hay*, and *Small Wonders* (eight of which have been book club selections); the illustrator of his own books; the writer of the syndicated column "A Lift for Living" and magazine articles which have appeared in *The Christian Herald, Church and Home*, and *The Reader's Digest*. Selections from his writings appear in anthologies of the world's wisdom and inspiration.

A lecturer in great demand, Dr. Kohn in 1963 was presented the Michigan Citizenship Award by Governor George Romney, having been selected as one of ten citizens who had given "distinguished leadership to the people of Michigan" in the preceding ten-year period.

His B.A. degree is from North Central College, Naperville, Illinois, and he did graduate work at the Evangelical Theological Seminary. The honorary degree of Doctor of Humane Letters was bestowed upon him by Olivet College.

Dr. Kohn and his wife Marian live at Hidden Brook, the forty-acre plot of birch, evergreen, and maple forest through which winds the small trout stream of which he writes so vividly and which gives the acreage its name. About five miles from the city of Charlevoix-the-Beautiful, the Kohn home is near both Lake Charlevoix and Lake Michigan, amidst the natural surroundings which he loves and the clear, clean air his health requires. The Kohns' daughter and son-in-law, Carolyn and Larry Minch, and grandsons Timmy and Kevin are frequent guests among the numerous visitors at Hidden Brook.

171

Hidden Brook